ISBN: 9781407753164

Published by:
HardPress Publishing
8345 NW 66TH ST #2561
MIAMI FL 33166-2626

Email: info@hardpress.net
Web: http://www.hardpress.net

I

THE LIFE AND TIMES

OF

GEN. JOHN GRAVES SIMCOE,

*Commander of the "Queen's Rangers" during the Revolutionary War,
and first Governor of Upper Canada,*

TOGETHER WITH

SOME ACCOUNT OF MAJOR ANDRE AND CAPT. BRANT

BY D. B. READ, Q.C.

*Historian of the County of York Law Association; Author of "The Lives of the
Judges of Upper Canada."*

TORONTO :

GEORGE VIRTUE, PUBLISHER.

1890.

PRINTED BY
C. BLACKETT ROBINSON
TORONTO.

DEDICATION.

To the People of Ontario:

Fellow Subjects,—I dedicate this book, "The Life and Times of General Simcoe, the First Governor of Upper Canada," to you. You are the natural guardians of the fame of the distinguished officer to whom was committed the destinies of Upper Canada when first severed from the Province of Quebec. Governor Simcoe, like many of the early settlers of the Province, was actively engaged on the British side in the American Revolutionary War. It was fitting that he should be the first Governor of a province the majority of whose people were his-compatriots. If the reading of this book should recall to your memory events of the past pleasant to be remembered and treasured up, it will afford gratification to no one more than to

Your humble servant,

THE AUTHOR.

January, 1890.

PREFACE.

THERE never yet has been published a history of the life of General Simcoe, the first Governor of Upper Canada. The pioneers of the country and their descendants are entitled to be made acquainted with the officer who was first entrusted with the administration of their affairs, and was the real founder of the Province. In writing " The Life and Times of General Simcoe" I have endeavoured to recall the public acts of the first Governor of Upper Canada in his different capacities of citizen, soldier and administrator. His career as a soldier and officer of the " Queen's Rangers " during the Revolutionary War naturally demands attention. For much that I have written on that subject I am indebted to the Journal which he himself kept during the different campaigns of the War of Independence. Regarding General Simcoe's career as Lieutenant-Governor I have availed myself of information gained from that valuable collection of manuscripts called " Smith's Papers," which the chief Librarian of the Public Library of Toronto so opportunely secured for that Institution.

Writing not only the memoirs, but a history of the times of Governor Simcoe, necessarily drew me a-field. The great Indian chief, Thayendanegea (Brant) was so intimate a friend of Simcoe, and held in such high regard, not only by the Governor, but by the people of the Province of Upper Canada, that I could not pass him over. I have given him a foremost place in the history of the Times.

The name of Major André, so familiar to those acquainted with the Revolutionary era, also finds a place in this history. His was a sad and undeserved fate, the recollection of which to this day rankles in many breasts.

I must not omit to mention that I have, in preparing this work, derived great assistance from the writings of Dr. Scadding, not only from his "Toronto of Old," but the " Memorial Volume," published to celebrate the Semi-Centennial of Toronto. I first satisfied myself that some record of the early times of the Province ought to be preserved, and acting upon this inspiration I set about writing this history which I now commit to the reading public, in the belief that its perusal will do no harm, and may do much good in reviving a memory of the past, and of the first era of a Province now the foremost of the Provinces of the Dominion of Canada.

CONTENTS.

CHAPTER IV.

Campaign of 1780.

CHAPTER V. ˋ

CAMPAIGN OF 1781.

CHAPTER VI.

Civil Government in Upper Canada.

CHAPTER VII.

THE FIRST PARLIAMENT OF UPPER CANADA.

CHAPTER VIII.

VISIT TO DETROIT AND THE MOHAWKS.

CHAPTER IX.

THE COMMISSIONERS' VISIT.

The King's Birthday, 4th June—How Observed—Governor's Ball—
American Commissioners at the Ball—Their description of the
dance, and the Civil and Military Guests—Their Praise of
the Canadian Ladies—Daughters of Sir William Johnson at
the Ball—Brant's Arrival at Fort Erie, and Meeting with the
American Commissioners—Conference of the Commissioners
and Indian Deputation at Navy Hall—Governor Simcoe and
a large number of Civil and Military Officers present—Brant
makes a Spirited Speech—Brant, the Commissioners and

CHAPTER X.

The Building of Fort Miami.

Road to Simcoe and Huron opened out—This Road now Yonge
Street—Governor Simcoe, in pursuance of directions of Lord
Dorchester, proceeds to Miami to Erect a Fort there—Danger-
ous and Difficult Enterprise—Succeeded in the Undertaking
—The American President writes to American Minister Jay
Protesting against this Invasion of American Territory—The
Erection of the Fort at Miami raised the hopes of the Indians
—The United States Superintendent of Indians and the
British Superintendent meet the Indians in Council—Captain
Brant's Eloquent Address to the Superintendents — Plain
Speaking—Brant Master Spirit not only of the Six Nations,
but of Confederacy of all the Indians—Another Indian War
looming up—Indian Council at Buffalo—Indians demand
removal of Settlers from their Lands—Indians charge Ameri-
can Government with Deception—Their Talk at Washington
—Brant's Letter to Colonel Smith for Governor Simcoe—
Indian Raid on Fort Recovery—Smith Manuscripts in Free

CHAPTER XI.

Establishing the Capital at York.

CHAPTER XII.

LAST DAYS IN CANADA.

CHAPTER XIII.

ST. DOMINGO AND THE PORTUGUESE MISSION.

List of Illustrations.

THE LIFE AND TIMES

OF

GEN. JOHN GRAVES SIMCOE.

CHAPTER I.

INTRODUCTION.—MILITARY CAREER.

NEARLY a hundred years have come and gone since the foundation of Upper Canada as a distinct Province was laid, yet up to this time there has never appeared a faithful account of the man who laid that foundation.

Lieut.-Colonel John Graves Simcoe was the son of John Graves Simcoe, Esq., who was Commander of His Majesty's ship *Pembroke*, and who lost his life in the Royal Service upon the important expedition against Quebec in the year 1759.

Though bred in the Navy the father of Governor Simcoe was equally well educated in the military service. The most striking occurrence of his life, it is said, arose from an accident, improved in a manner

peculiar to genius and extensive professional knowledge. The story is that he was taken prisoner by
the French, in America, and carried up the St. Lawrence. As his character was little known he was
watched only to prevent his escape ; but from his
observations on his voyage to Quebec, and the little
incidental information he was able to obtain, he constructed a chart of that river, and was able to conduct
General Wolfe in his famous attack upon the Canadian capital.

Soon after Simcoe's father was killed his mother
took up her residence at Exeter, in England, and
while living there she sent her young son, John
Graves, who afterwards so distinguished himself in
several capacities, both military and civil, to the Free
Grammar School of that town. At the age of fourteen he was removed to Eton, and from thence, in
due course, to Merton College, Oxford. While a
schoolboy at the Free Grammar School in Exeter
his acquisitions in some departments of knowledge
were of a superior kind. He was devoted to the
study of ancient and modern literature. He was
well versed in modern history, and eagerly devoured
every tale of war. Before leaving the University
he had mastered Tacitus and Xenophon, ever after
his constant friends and companions, whether in the
study or on the tented field. At the age of nineteen

he obtained an Ensign's commission in the 35th Regiment. This regiment was sent to America, being one of the many regiments sent from England for the purpose of quelling the rebellion of the American Provinces. Ensign Simcoe did not embark from England with his regiment, but he landed at Boston on the memorable day of the Battle of Bunker's Hill, 17th June, 1775. Shortly after this event he purchased command of a company in the 40th Regiment, which he led at the Battle of Brandywine, where the British Commander, Sir William Howe, defeated General Washington and became master of the City of Philadelphia.

The Battle of Brandywine was fought on the 11th day of September, 1777, and was hotly contested by the British troops of the line and Provincials. Captain Simcoe, in command of a company in the 40th Regiment, distinguished himself in the engagement, and Sir William Howe was not only pleased with the success of his army, but thought the occasion one deserving of special honour. The Queen's Rangers, a provincial corps which took part in this engagement, lost a great many men, both officers and soldiers. They performed most essential service in gaining the victory of the day, and this induced the Commander, Sir William Howe, to promise them that all promotions should go with the regiment. Shortly after this affair, on the 15th October, 1777, Sir William Howe was pleased to appoint Captain Simcoe, of the regular service, who was then of the Grenadiers, with the provincial rank of Major, to the command of the Queen's Rangers. The next day he joined the regiment, which was .encamped with the army in the vicinity of Germantown, close to Philadelphia. It is matter of history that the Americans made an effort to retrieve their fortune, after their defeat at Brandywine and capture of the City of Philadelphia, by an attack on Germantown, but were repulsed with loss.

The Queen's Rangers, to which Captain Simcoe had been appointed Major, were originally raised in Connecticut and the vicinity of New York, by Colonel Rogers, and their duties, which indeed their name implies, were principally those of scouts or light cavalry. At one time the Rangers mustered four hundred men, all Americans, and all Loyalists. When Major Simcoe joined the regiment, it had by hardships and neglect been reduced in numbers ; many gentlemen of the southern colonies, who had joined Lord Dunmore and distinguished themselves under his orders, were appointed to supersede those who were not competent for the commissions they had hitherto borne. To these were added some volunteers from the army, the whole consisting of young men, active, full of love of the service, emulous to distinguish themselves in it, and looking forward to obtain through their actions the honour of being enrolled with the British army.

The Queen's Rangers was in many respects an exceptional regiment, having privileges not accorded to other corps. It was an irregular, independent and mixed corps. They were not regular cavalrymen, but took the place of what would now be called mounted infantry. The regiment was principally composed of light horsemen, but had attached companies of light infantry, and was specially organized for rapid movements, and irregular outposts and skirmishing. The cavalry detachment went under the name of the Queen's Rangers Hussars, composed of men from the corps, who with care and attention became most skilled horsemen.

The origin of this branch of the regiment arose in this way. Shortly after Major Simcoe joined the regiment, upon the march from Germantown to Kensington, Sir William Erskine, in directing what Major Simcoe's duties should be, had told him to call upon him for dragoons whenever he wanted them ; upon this, Major Simcoe took the liberty of observing "that the clothing and habiliments of the dragoons were so different from those of the Queen's Rangers (the one being in red and with white belts, easily seen in the distance, and the other in green and accoutred for concealment), that he thought it would be more useful to mount a dozen soldiers of the regiment."

A dozen soldiers was a very small force of cavalry to be attached to a regiment which was principally occupied in outpost duty and skirmishing, making expeditions over the whole region of coast country extending from the Chesapeake to Long Island. But as the war continued, the Hussars were increased to as many as sixty, which, I believe, was the full complement of this portion of the regiment.

While the British army in America was quartered in New York there was published in *Rimington's Royal Gazette*, in that city, an advertisement which no doubt assisted greatly in adding to the effective strength of the Hussars. The advertisement was as follows :—

"ALL ASPIRING HEROES

Have now an opportunity of distinguishing themselves
by joining

THE QUEEN'S RANGERS HUZZARS,

Commanded by

LIEUTENANT-COLONEL SIMCOE.

"Any spirited young man will receive every encouragement, be immediately mounted on an elegant horse, and furnished with clothing, accoutrements, etc., to the amount of FORTY GUINEAS, by applying to Cornet Spencer, at his quarters, No. 1033 Water Street, or his rendezvous, Hewitt's

Tavern, near the Coffee House, and the depot at Brandy-wine, on Golden Hill.

"☞ Whoever brings a Recruit shall instantly receive TWO GUINEAS.

"VIVANT REX ET REGINA ! "

It will be observed that the recruiting officer did not fail to add the name of Queen as well as King to his advertisement, mindful, no doubt, that the regiment was *The Queen's Rangers.* Different from other regiments, the Queen's Rangers were almost exclusively at the command of their own commanding officer. It was understood that the regiment was always, and at all times, to be ready to strike a blow wherever they were most needed against the continental rebels, as those were called who, in arms, espoused the cause of the revolutionary Americans. To do this effectually, it was most essential that the corps should have full and complete liberty of action, and they had liberty to do or die in the service, without waiting for all the formalities of red tape and orders from the Commander-in-Chief. If the colonel of the regiment should at any time suggest an enterprise, however hazardous, but which, in his opinion, could be successfully undertaken, it was expected that his superior officer would sanction the duty without hesitation or reserve.

In the *Pennsylvania Newspaper*, of December 3rd, 1777, was printed the following notice :—" No regiment in the army has gained more honour in the campaign than Major Weys's (or the Queen's) Rangers; they have been engaged in every principal service, and behaved nobly ; indeed, most of the officers have been wounded, since we took the field in· Pennsylvania. General Knifhausen, after the action of the 11th September, at Brandywine, despatched an aide-de-camp to General Howe with an account of it. What he said was short but to the purpose. ' Tell the General,' said he, ' I must be silent as to the behaviour of the Rangers, for I even want words to express my astonishment to give an idea of it.' "

On the 13th the following appeared in orders :— " The Commander-in-Chief desires to convey to the officers and men of the Queen's Rangers his approbation and acknowledgment for their spirited and gallant behaviour in the engagement of the 11th instant, and to assure them how well he is satisfied with their distinguished conduct on that day. His Excellency only regrets their having suffered so much in the gallant execution of their duty."

Throughout the whole war the Queen's Rangers were subject to most severe duties and were ever ready and anxious to perform any service which might be of benefit to the king's cause. They were quick in action, vigilant in performance of duty; of great endurance and undoubted courage. During the course of a week the Infantry would often march ninety miles, and the Hussars many more. They were penetrating and observant, skilled in ambuscade and stratagem, just the kind of corps suited to a country of wood and stream, of which they always endeavoured to make pitfalls for the enemy. There was a company of Highlanders added to the regiment, commanded by a most excellent officer, Captain McKay, who, like most Highlanders, did noble service for the King in the different campaigns which the Queen's Rangers went through. Before the war was over there was an accession to the regiment of an Irish company which added materially to the strength of the regiment. It was one of the privileges which the Queen's Rangers had, that when by the fortunes of war, death or disease, the regiment became reduced, the commanding officer, in order to fill up the ranks, was entitled to enlist Old Countrymen (as Europeans were termed in America) and deserters from the rebel army; so that were the officers, to whom the Commander-in-Chief delegated the inspection of the Provincial Corps able to execute their orders, the Queen's Rangers, however dangerously and incessantly employed, would never be in want of recruits; at the same time the major part of the regiment was made up of the native born Loyalists. The regiment, at its full strength, did not number more than five hundred and fifty Infantry, and yet was one of

the most effective in the service.   There were as
many as twenty-seven other Provincial Corps of Loyalists who, no doubt, did excellent service, but as the
Queen's Rangers was a flying column, specially
detailed for outpost duty and roaming at large over
the whole country, they were brought more into notice
and were more prominent than other regiments which
were raised to defend the loyal cause during the Revolution.   It has been said of this corps "that no sentinel
or guard of the Queen's Rangers was ever surprised"—
the reason given is that sergeant's guards were in a
manner abolished, the guard duty being principally
performed by the commissioned officers of the corps.
It would occupy too much time, to give a complete
account of the life of Major Simcoe while attached to
the Queen's Rangers, or a detailed description of all
the engagements in which his regiment was engaged
during the War of Independence, but it may be allow-
able and pardonable to dwell at some length upon the
memoirs of an officer who, on more than one occasion, received the thanks of his superiors in the
service, and of his King and country.   It will be
convenient to divide up his military service into campaigns, and as he joined the Queen's Rangers late
in 1777, the campaign of 1777–1778 may well be
described as a notable period of his military life.

CHAPTER II.

THE CAMPAIGNS OF 1777-1778.

THE headquarters of the British Army in October, 1777, was at Philadelphia. The Queen's Rangers were posted about four miles from Philadelphia, on the road leading to Frankfort, a village on Frankfort Creek, about five miles from headquarters. It was there Major Simcoe first met the Polish officer Pulaski, in command of the Continental troops in that district. The opposing troops did not, however, come to close quarters, though it was thought that an encounter might take place at or in the vicinity of Frankfort. On the 3rd of November, 1777, the very distressing news came from New York that General Burgoyne's army on their march from Ticonderoga (which they had reduced) had reached Saratoga, where, being surrounded by the American forces, he was compelled to surrender to the American generals, Gates and Arnold, and that his troops were made prisoners of war. Such news, at such a time, read in general orders to the Rangers on their parade, was very dispiriting indeed to the officers, and might have proved disastrous, were it not for the temper and spirit the men displayed on the distressing occasion. When Major Simcoe came to one of the articles of surrender proposed by the American generals, rejected by General Burgoyne's army in the following terms :— " Sooner than this army will consent to ground their arms in their encampment they will rush on the enemy determined to take no quarter," the whole corps thrilled with animation and resentment against the enemy, and every soldier of the regiment burned to revenge the insult put upon him by the Revolutionists.

It was always the policy of Major Simcoe to conciliate the people of the country as much as was in his power. In a civil war, where the masses divide in their allegiance, it often becomes difficult to distinguish friend from foe. The nearest relatives and nearest neighbours are often in opposing camps. In the campaigning around Philadelphia, he found many of the people well disposed towards the British, and to continue their friendliness it was necessary that the Rangers should afford them protection. Protection means abstaining from plundering and marauding. Consequently we find Major Simcoe very early in the campaign warning his force against this evil. When a general order was given out, enforcing the regulation to which I have referred, Major Simcoe felt bound to declare "that it is with the utmost satisfaction Major Simcoe believes there would have been no necessity for the general orders of this day had every corps of the army been as regular in respect to their abstaining from plunder and marauding as the Rangers. He trusts that so truly a military behaviour will be continued, and that the officer and soldier of the corps will consider it as honourable to him as the most distinguished bravery."

To illustrate the method adopted by Major Simcoe to prevent plundering, it may be noticed that on the march he never halted, if he could avoid it, but in a wood ; sent a safeguard to every house ; allowed no man to leave the ranks ; and was careful to instil into the minds of the men the belief that while they protected the country the inhabitants would give every information of the enemy's movements and ambuscades. At the close of the campaign of 1777 an attempt was made at headquarters to have the military dress of the Queen's Rangers changed from green to red. This move was opposed by Major Simcoe, his opinion being that green with dark accoutrements is beyond comparison the best colour for light infantry uniforms.

In the campaign of 1778 the first we hear of Major Simcoe is that about the end of February he and the Rangers were employed in opposing the force

of General Wayne, who had been detached from
Washington's army to make a forage in the lower
Jerseys in order to collect cattle for provisioning the
troops.   This expedition was not as successful as it
might have been had the views which Major Simcoe
entertained of the proper time and place for attack
been followed.   After crossing the Delaware an
incident occurred reflecting honour equally upon the
Queen's Rangers and on a Polish officer in the
American service.   As related by Major Simcoe the
incident was this :   At a certain point there was
nothing opposed to the Rangers but some cavalry
watching their motions, and as Major Simcoe advanced rapidly to gain an eminence in front, which
he conceived to be a strong advantageous position,
tion, they fled into the wood, an officer excepted, who,
reining back his horse, and fronting the Rangers as
they advanced, slowly waved with his sword for his
attendants to retire ; the light infantry being within
fifty yards of him, they called out to him, "You are a
brave fellow, but you must go away."   But he not
paying so much attention as he should, McGill, afterwards quarter-master, was directed to fire at him, on
which he retired into the woods.   A few straggling
shots were fired in the front ; the light infantry company was detached there, and, supported by the Highlanders, soon cleared the front ; the battalion halted

on the position it had gained, and at the entreaties of the sailors, a few cannon shot were fired at a party of the enemy who were near the bridge over Cooper's Creek, till perceiving they were busy in destroying it, they were no longer interrupted; the firing totally ceased, and the enemy retreated. The person whom McGill fired at proved to be Pulaski; his horse was wounded, and had not the Hussars been sent over the Delaware previous to the attack, he would have been taken or killed.

We are now in March, 1778, Simcoe, still Major, but the regiment was commanded by Colonel Mawhood. All the honour of the campaign must not, therefore, be given to Major Simcoe, for although he and his band had to perform much executive duty, the Colonel of the Regiment directed the movements on the field. This was especially the case in a successful expedition of the Queen's Rangers and other corps into the Jerseys in the latter part of March, 1778. This expedition was formed to forage for horses for the cavalry and staff, the army being very deficient in this branch of the service; the expedition was to be made on a strip of land on the Jersey side of the Delaware, between two creeks near Salem. The country between the two streams (the Salem Creek and Aloes or Alewas Creek) is a peninsula seven miles wide at the widest part and four miles wide at the narrowest part. Over the Aloes Creek there were three bridges : Hancock's, near the mouth ; Quintin's, the next higher up, and Thompson's above that. The rebel militia was posted at Hancock's and Quintin's, the nearest bridges, which they had destroyed, and was in a favourable position and defended by breastworks. The object of the continentals was to prevent the expedition crossing the creek, and to cut them off if they should retreat.

Under the orders of Col. Mawhood, Major Simcoe silently placed a company of the Rangers under Captain Stephenson in possession of a public-house near Quintin's bridge, and stationed the men in an orchard in rear of the house, two companies of the Rangers being placed in ambuscade, behind some fences at the edge of the wood, near the public-house. The Colonel then gave orders for a detachment of the 17th Regiment, which was posted near the bridge, to call in their sentries and retreat up the road in full view of the enemy. This so completely deceived the rebel forces that they hastily re-laid the bridge across the stream, and crossing it marched up the road past the house in which the Rangers were concealed. Suddenly they discovered they had fallen into a trap, and made an effort to retreat and re-cross the creek. When passing the house the Rangers rushed out and drove them across the fields ; Captain Saunders pursued them, and the Hussars were despatched in pursuit, and afterwards the battalion, Colonel Mawhood leading them. Major Simcoe now directed the 17th back to the house, with the Grenadiers, and the Highlanders of the Rangers, ready to force the bridge if ordered. The enemy for a moment quitted it, but Col. Mawhood thought it useless to pass it. Some of the division of rebels who passed the house were taken prisoners, but the greater part were drowned in the Aloes Creek. The officer at the head of the division, who was taken prisoner, proved to be a Frenchman. The victorious Rangers then returned to Salem.

The rebels still occupying posts at Quintin and Hancock's Bridge, Colonel Mawhood determined to attack them at the latter place. Near Hancock's Bridge, from all reports, they were assembled nearly four hundred strong. He entrusted the enterprise to Major Simcoe, and before the expedition set out went with him and a patrol to a point opposite to the place where the rebels were posted. Here the Major ascended a tree and made a rough sketch of the buildings, and by conversing with the guides he was able to improve it into a tolerable plan of the place, and formed his mode of attack accordingly. In this enterprise everything depended on secrecy and surprise. Major Simcoe foresaw the difficulties and dangers; these he kept to himself. The enemy were nearly double his numbers. By an order that had been issued for the destruction of the flat-boats he had made use of in making a landing on the creek, his retreat, if he should be obliged to make one, was cut off. Nothing daunted, however, he, with his brave soldiers, by dint of hard work, after a march of two miles through marshes, up to the knees in mud and water, their labours rendered the more fatiguing by their carrying wooden planks for the construction of bridges over the creeks and ditches, at length arrived at a point where they obtained the shelter of a wood, made the intended attack, captured the position of the enemy, and came off entirely victorious. The result of these well-planned and successful expeditions was that the foragers got all the cattle they wanted for the supply of the troops, and what proved very satisfactory to the people of the country whose cattle had been taken, when the object of the expedition had been accomplished, they were fully paid for the losses which the necessities of civil war had entailed upon them.

Colonel Mawhood after this affair, in public orders, "returned his best thanks to Major Simcoe and his corps for their spirited and good conduct in the surprise of the rebel posts." The foraging expedition having ended, the troops returned to Philadelphia, after which nothing of importance transpired while Simcoe was major of the regiment.

No long time elapsed before news reached Philadelphia that Sir William Howe, the then Commander-in-chief, had been recalled and Sir Henry Clinton took command of the army. Major Simcoe was now appointed Lieutenant-Colonel of the Queen's Rangers. This was brought about in this way : Sir Henry Clinton, when he took command, directed Lord Rawdon to raise a corps of Irish volunteers, and Captain Doyle, of the 55th Regiment, was appointed Lieutenant-Colonel. Major Simcoe waited upon the Commander-in-chief, and requested that, as he was Captain Doyle's senior in the army, he would be pleased to give him his proper position in the Provincial line, adding that if his Excellency, at any future time, should appoint a senior officer of the line to a Provincial command, he, Major Simcoe, of course could have no objection that he should have superior rank in the Provinces. Sir Henry Clinton was pleased to refer his request to Sir William Erskine and General Patterson, the Quartermaster and Adjutant-General, who reporting that it was just, Sir Henry Clinton appointed him to the rank of Lieutenant-Colonel, and to avoid similar inconveniences, ante-dated his commission to those of all other Provincial lieutenant-colonels.

On the 17th of June, 1778, Lieutenant-Colonel Simcoe observed in public orders " that he doubted not but that all ranks of the regiment were sensible that the undaunted spirit which had rendered them the terror of their enemies was not more honourable to them than that abhorrence of plunder which distinguishes the truly brave from the cowardly ruffian, and which had left a favourable impression on the minds of such of the inhabitants of Pennsylvania as had been in their power." He assured himself that, as they were to pass over to the Jerseys, they would, in every respect, behave as became the character the corps had acquired, and which marks the disciplined soldier. He gave orders that the captains and officers commanding companies should march in the rear of their respective divisions till such time as more active duties required their presence elsewhere, and should be answerable that no soldier quitted his rank on any pretence, but *particularly to drink* ; this practice having been the death of many a valuable soldier, the permission of it was highly criminal.

The man who could issue such an order at such a time was no ordinary man. The very words of the order seem to say in trumpet tones that Lieutenant-Colonel Simcoe was every inch a soldier and had all the characteristics of the British officer of the old school—honour, integrity, courage and capacity. This was the man who led the Queen's Rangers in time of danger ; who, when the toils of war were over, settled down peacefully in Upper Canada as Governor

of the Province, surrounded by many of his old com-
rades, who with him had shared the fatigues of many
campaigns and who, ever ready to serve their country,
rose *en masse* in defence of the Province when in the
war of 1812 it was invaded and thrown into convulsion
by a foe who chose to challenge them to conflict in an
unjust war.

On the 24th June, 1778, we find the army on
the march from Philadelphia pursuing their course
northward, with now and then a skirmish with the
enemy on the line of march. Hitherto the direction of
the march pointed equally to Trenton, New Jersey,
or Cranberry, but now, on the 24th, took the route
to Cranberry, by marching to Allentown. The Rangers
formed the advance of the army, and it happened more
than once that the patriots of the continent were
deceived by the uniform of the Rangers being green—
the same as their own—and mistaking foe for friend.
One episode of this kind occurred at the camp when
the army halted not far from Allentown. It happened
in this manner : On the arrival at the camp Lieutenant-
Colonel Simcoe, with his Hussars, immediately explored
a deep hollow that separated the camping-ground from
a high hill, in order to observe the ground in front, as
was his constant custom. Two men came out of the
wood to Lieutenant Wickham, who was patrolling,
deceived by his green clothes ; he did not undeceive

them, but passed himself upon them as a rebel partizan, and introduced Lieutenant-Colonel Simcoe as the American Colonel Lee. One of the men was very glad to see him, and told him that he had a son in his corps, and gave him the best account of the movement of the rebel army, from which Lieutenant-Colonel Simcoe said he had been detached two days. The other man proved to be a committeeman of New Jersey. They pointed out the encampment of the British army, and were completely deceived till, having told all they knew, and, on the party returning, the committeeman having asked, " I wonder what Clinton is about ? " " You shall ask him yourself," was the answer, " for we are British."

This was as complete a *ruse de guerre* as could be conceived. In reading the history of these campaigns I have found that both armies often resorted to stratagem for the effecting of their purpose. Owing to the situation and the topography of the country, ambuscades, surprises and stratagems were frequently resorted to. It is to be borne in mind that the country was a country of wood, water-courses, cross-roads, marsh, and of a very uneven character. Many of the country people were rebels at heart, and often shewed themselves in active hostility to the British army in their progress northward, making for New York and Long Island. On the other hand there were many

Loyalists in the country, who demanded and received protection from the King's troops. These Loyalists, often in great numbers, had to betake themselves to the British camp, to escape the vengeance of their republican neighbours ; they passed under the name of refugees, and frequently accepted service in the British army as scouts and guides. Indeed, being much impoverished by the war, they were willing to undertake various duties more difficult than agreeable, which was the natural outcome of civil war.

In the march through New Jersey, Colonel Simcoe seems to have received his first wound. This was on the 27th June, 1778, when he met, in front of battle, Baron Steuben, of the American army, and a force of the Jersey Militiamen, 700 or 800 strong, under General Dickenson. It was in this affair that Simcoe, anxious about his Grenadiers, who had been placed at a certain exposed place, sent forward a Hussar to ascertain how they fared, and said to the Hussar, in giving him his charge, to find out what the fact was, " For we must carry them off or lie with them ;" to which the Hussar replied, " *To be sure, your honour.*" This reply would seem to show that some Irish had got into the Hussars. It has been said that, " The American War shewed no instance of a larger body of men discomfited by so small a number" as in this engagement with the Jersey Militia. The Grenadier Company of the Queen's Rangers were mostly Hessians. Lieutenant-Colonel Simcoe, after the encounter with the Jersey Militia, to which I have referred, heard a person, who was of the American force, call the Grenadier's Company of the Rangers, to use his own expression, " A power of Hessians;" which form of expression establishes, pretty clearly, that the Americans were not without their contingent of American Irishmen. The fact is that there were foreigners in both armies : in the English army some Hessians, in the American, German and French. The Baron Steuben, with the Jersey Militia, was a German, and it is known that the French allies of the Americans, under the Marquis de Lafayette, contributed most materially to the success of the American army in the Revolution. It is indeed doubtful if the American Revolutionists would have gained their independence if they had not had the assistance of French soldiers and French officers, who had been schooled in the art of war in meeting English troops in other fields.

In the summer of 1778 the Commander-in-Chief, Sir Henry Clinton, offered to promote Lieut.-Col. Simcoe to the Colonelcy of the Queen's Rangers, but he declined the promotion.

On the 20th August, 1778, Lieut.-Col. Simcoe was at Kingston, where he and Lieut.-Col. Tarleton with the cavalry had a skirmish with the rebel light infantry and a body of Indians, forty of whom were killed or desperately wounded; among others, Niniham, 'a chieftain, who had been in England, and his son. This discomfiture of the Indians was reported to have prevented a large portion of them from joining General Washington's army. The Indian doctor was taken, and he said that when Niniham saw the Grenadiers close in his rear he called out to his people to fly, "that he himself would die there." He wounded Simcoe and was killed by Wright, his orderly Hussar. On the 31st August, 1778, Simcoe and the Rangers made another attack on the enemy at Kingsbridge and succeeded in the attack, for soon after this General Washington quitted the White Plains, where he had been quartered. Simcoe was much gratified when the country people attributed the departure of General Washington to the continued checks which his light troops had received at the hands of the Rangers.

After the successes that Lieut.-Col. Simcoe had had at Kingsbridge he and his brave troops were entitled to a rest. The season had for some time been very inclement, and was severely felt by the troops encamped on the exposed heights of Kingsbridge. It was therefore with great pleasure that they received orders to march to winter quarters at Oyster Bay, on Long Island, where they arrived on the 19th November. Immediately on their arrival the troops set to work to fully fortify the position. The New England shore, from which the British expected attack, was not more than twelve, and in many places but seven or eight, miles distant, and there were many favourable landing places within a mile or two of Oyster Bay. Every precaution was taken by Simcoe to prevent an attack, and he had the satisfaction of hearing, after the war was over, that his precautions were not in vain, for more than once an attack on Oyster Bay was contemplated, and the project as often discarded, the enemy fearing to risk an attack on his fortified position.

The spirit of the Queen's Rangers was well shewn while they were stationed at Oyster Bay. Recruits were wanted for the regiment, whom they would have had difficulty in procuring, (as much greater bounties were being given by other regiments then being raised than Government allowed for the provincial corps) had not the officers of the regiment subscribed liberally to the recruiting fund from their own scanty pay.

The garrison of New York being in great want of forage, Oyster Bay now became a central and safe depôt for it, and frequent expeditions, toward the eastern and interior parts of the island, were made to enforce the order of the Commander-in-Chief to secure the necessary supply. Other excursions were also frequently made to execute orders relative to the intercourse with the inhabitants of the rebel coast.

There were a number of whale-boats of the enemy at Norwalk, on the New England coast. The Queen's Rangers would have liked to have been given a chance to burn these boats, but the proposal being submitted to the Commander-in-Chief, he did not think it advisable to put the plan into execution. This was disappointing to the corps, as the officers always understood that whatever plans they might offer for the good of the King's service would be considered and fairly dealt with by the Commander-in-Chief, and that they should be allowed to reap the fruit of their own exertions.

During the winter the regiment was kept at very constant drill. The light infantry and hussars were put under the direction of Captain Saunders, who taught them to gallop through woods, and, acting together, the light infantry learned to run, holding the horses' manes. The cavalry was also instructed, as the infantry lay flat on the ground, to gallop through their files. When the weather permitted, the corps was frequently exercised together, particularly in occupying ground, on the supposition of the enemy landing to attack the post ; they were shown how to make and navigate rafts, constructed on the simplest principles and with the lightest materials.

It is impossible to withhold from the Queen's Rangers in the campaign of 1777-1778 great praise for their vigilance, promptness in action, patience under trying duties and general discipline, all of which tended to make them not only good, but successful soldiers, an honour to themselves and to the country which bore them.   Lieutenant-Colonel Simcoe felt it to be an honour to have the command of such a regiment. When he left the regular service he did so with the ambition to be at the head of a Provincial corps which he could mould to his will.   There never was a body of men more devoted to their commanding officer than were the Rangers to Simcoe.   He showed his appreciation of their services in the most marked manner. His pride was that they were Loyalists of a country in rebellion, and were imbued with all those high principles of attachment.to their sovereign begotten of the feeling in their breasts that the rebellion of the Colonists was without sufficient cause ; that the blame for unremedied grievances lay at the door of the Ministry, not at that of the King, and that with more peaceful times the clouds which overhung the continent would be cleared away and a sunshine of contentment cover the land.

CHAPTER III.

CAMPAIGN OF 1779.

THE last chapter concluded the campaign of 1777-1778, and we now enter on the campaign of 1779. I mentioned two instances in the last chapter where foraging expeditions were undertaken, the one to seize horses, the other to seize other live stock for provisioning the troops. The campaign of 1779 opened with an expedition of another sort, and was undertaken to seize men. I have before mentioned that many of the Loyalists, not in the service, either regular or Provincial, frequently fled from their homes to claim the protection of the British army. The Queen's Rangers was a favourite regiment for them to appeal to, there being so many sons of the soil in that regiment—not a few friends and relatives, their neighbours when at home following their peaceful pursuits. Such persons, when they became in a manner enrolled, were called " Refugees." On the 18th of April a party of Refugees went from Oyster Bay, being furnished with arms, agreeably to an order from headquarters, to take the American Generals Parsons and Silliman from the opposite shore, in fact, to endeavour to kidnap these two prominent officers of the enemy. They did not risk the attack on General Parsons, but they brought Brigadier Silliman to Oyster Bay, and he was sent the next day to New York.

The Provincial troops received in May of this year a signal mark of the royal favour, which must have been particularly gratifying to them, as an acknowledgment of the services they had rendered to the crown in time of danger. On the 2nd of May the Commander-in-Chief was pleased to signify, in general orders to the Provincial troops, "that his Majesty, anxious to reward their faithful services and spirited conduct, upon several occasions, has been pleased to confer upon them the following mark of his royal favour" : The articles were then enumerated, and were all material to that service. The principal were: " That the officers of Provincial corps shall rank as juniors of the rank to which they belong, and if disabled in service should be entitled to the same gratuity as officers of the established army ; and to distinguish the zeal of such as shall be completed, his Majesty will, upon the recommendation of the Commander-in-Chief, make the rank of those officers permanent in America, and will allow them half pay, upon the reduction of their regiments, in the same manner as the officers of the British reduced regiments are paid."

In consequence of this order the Queen's Rangers were recommended by the Commander-in-Chief, and styled and numbered as the "First American Regiment."

Early in June we find Simcoe at Croton Bridge, having marched to that place for the purpose of recapturing cattle which the enemy had seized upon, the property of people in the neighbourhood. At the same time, he covered the retreat of Lieut.-Col. Tarleton, of the Legion, who had passed that bridge and beat up the quarters of a party, four miles further.

During the struggle for Independence, as is well known, there were regular troops as well as militia on both sides. An army marching through the country had to be especially watchful or they would be sure to fall into an ambush or ambuscade of some sort. Each party was always looking out for stragglers from the other in the hope, by force or persuasion, to win them over to their cause. The Queen's Rangers had, up to the 10th of July of this year, 1779, been particularly fortunate in keeping well in hand. They seldom afforded an opportunity to the enemy to capture them individually or in squads. A misfortune of this kind, however, did happen to the corps on the day above mentioned, in their march from Byram's Bridge to Marmaroneck. Upon this march three soldiers straggled a small distance from their ranks and were taken by some of the enemy's militia. This occurrence gave great concern to Simcoe and was the first of the kind that had happened. He thought it necessary to give a gentle rebuke to the corps in consequence of it, by a general order, in which he said :—" The Lieutenant-Colonel is most sensibly affected at the loss of the three men who straggled from their posts during the last march. He feels himself but ill repaid for the confidence he has placed in the regiment, and his inclination to ease their duty by never posting an unnecessary sentinel ; at the same time he trusts that as it has been the *first instance* of the kind during the time that he has had the honour of commanding the Queen's Rangers it will be the last ; and that the soldiers will reflect what they must suffer by a long imprisonment from a mean and despicable enemy, who never has or can gain any' advantage over them but what arises from their own disobedience of orders."

This order not only shews the high appreciation the Lieutenant-Colonel had of his own corps, but the contempt he felt for the enemy. Lieut.-Col. Simcoe was one of those officers desperately in love with the service ; he entered the Provincial Royalist force because of the strong belief he entertained that the Continentals had rebelled without cause, and that they never could or would succeed in their revolution. Time has shown how mistaken he was in this ; but this does not in the least detract from his honour or that of his regiment as soldiers in the King's service, however much it may detract from his prescience as a man. He was not alone in the belief of the Royalists of the day, that the Americans would not obtain their independence as a Republican nation, or if they did that they could not maintain their autonomy.

But to follow the Queen's Rangers. On the 8th August, after recapturing a number of the peaceful country Loyalists, who had been seized by the enemy, the light troops fell back on the redoubts. A grand guard being in advance, which reported to Lieut.-Col. Simcoe as senior officer of the Provincials, the Queen's Rangers were for the first time since they left winter quarters permitted to take off their coats each night until further orders. In case of sudden alarm they were ordered to form on their company's parade, with silence and regularity, without delaying to dress, and their bayonets were never to be unfixed. On the 9th October the Queen's Rangers were ordered to be in readiness to embark at the shortest notice. They immediately marched to Richmond, on Staten Island, where they relieved a regiment which had been sickly while at that post.

At the end of October Lieut.-Col. Simcoe and the Rangers were engaged in an enterprise which had the sanction of the Commander-in-Chief, Sir

Henry Clinton. This was to march into the Jerseys and over-awe the rebels who were giving countenance and support to Washington's army. Lieut.-Col. Simcoe had the impression that fifty flat boats, upon carriages, capable of holding fifty men each, were on the road from Delaware to Washington's army, and that they had been collected together at Van-Vacter's bridge upon the Rariton. It was important, if this information was correct, that these flat-boats should be captured. Stratagem had to be resorted to effect the purpose; and Lieut.-Col. Simcoe set about it, and succeeded in accomplishing all that was necessary for the security of his troops and the discomfiture of the enemy. On the 25th October, by eight o'clock at night, the detachment, which had been detailed for the service, marched to Billop's Point, where they were to embark. That the object of the enterprise might be effectually concealed, Lieut.-Col. Simcoe gave out that a rebel spy was on the Island (Staten Island), and was endeavouring to escape to New Jersey; a great reward was offered for taking him, and the militia of the Island were watching all the places where it was possible for any man to leave the Island, in order to apprehend him. The batteaux and boats, which were to be at Billop's Point, so as to pass the whole over by twelve o'clock at night, did not arrive till three o'clock in the morning. No time was lost; the infantry of the Queen's Rangers were landed ; they ambuscaded every avenue to the town, the cavalry following as fast as possible. As soon as they had formed in position Simcoe called together the officers ; he told them of his plan, which was to burn the boats at Van-Vacter's bridge, and crossing the Rariton at Hillsborough, to return by the road to Brunswick, and making a circuit to avoid that place as soon as he came near it, to discover himself when beyond it in the heights where the Grenadier Redoubt stood while the British troops were cantoned there and where the Queen's Rangers had afterwards been encamped ; and to entice the Militia, if possible, to follow him into ambuscade which the Infantry would lay for them at South River Bridge.

Major Armstrong was instructed to re-embark, as soon as the cavalry marched, and to land on the opposite side of the Rariton and South Amboy. He was then, with the utmost dispatch and silence, to proceed to South River bridge, six miles from South Amboy, where he was to ambuscade himself, without passing the bridge or taking it up. A smaller creek falls into this river on the South Amboy side. Into the peninsula formed by these streams Lieut.-Col. Simcoe hoped to allure the Jersey militia. In case of accident, Major Armstrong was desired to give credit to any messenger who should give him the parole of "Clinton and Montrose." It was daybreak before the cavalry left Amboy.

The procuring of guides had been entrusted by Sir Henry Clinton to Brigadier Skinner. He either did not or could not obtain them, for but one was found who knew perfectly the crossroad he meant to take, to avoid the main road from Somerset Court House, or Hillsborough to Brunswick.

Captain Sandford formed the advance guard, the Hussars followed, and Stuart's men were in the rear, making in the whole about eighty. A certain Justice Crow was soon overtaken ; Lieut.-Col. Simcoe accosted him roughly, called him " Tory," nor seemed to believe his excuses when he said "he had only been sparking," but sent him to the rear guard, who, being Americans, easily comprehended their instructions, and kept the Justice to the belief that the party was a detachment from Washington's army. Many plantations were now passed, the inhabitants of which were up, and these the party accosted with friendly salutations. At Quibletown Lieut.-Col. Simcoe had just quitted the advance guard to speak to Lieut. Stuart, when from a public house on the turn of the road, some people came out with knapsacks on their shoulders, bearing the appearance of a rebel guard. Captain Sandford did not see them till he had passed by, when checking his horse to give notice, the Hussars were reduced to a momentary halt opposite the house. Perceiving the supposed guard, they threw themselves off their horses, sword in hand, and entered the house. Lieut.-Col. Simcoe instantly made them re-mount, as he was afraid to delay so that they could search for some thousand pounds of paper-money which had been taken from a traveller, the master of a privateer, by the previous visitors. In order to let the man suppose he was of the same party he told him "that he would be answerable to give him his money that night at Brunswick, where he should quarter," then exclaimed aloud to his party "that these were not the Tories they were in search of, although they had knapsacks," and told the country people who were assembling round "that a party of Tories had made their escape from Sullivan's army, and were ready to get into Staten Island, as Jeff (who had been defeated near this very spot, taken and executed) had formerly done, and that he was sent to intercept them." The sight of Justice Crow would probably have aided in deceiving the inhabitants, but unfortunately a man who personally knew Lieut.-Col. Simcoe recognized him, and an express was sent to Governor Livingston, then at Brunswick, as soon as the party marched. It was now conducted by a country lad whom they fell in with, and to whom Captain Sandford, being dressed in red and without his cloak, had been introduced as a French officer. He gave information that the greater part of the boats had been sent on to Washington's camp, but that eighteen were at Van-Vacter's bridge, and that their horses were at a farm about a mile from it. He led the party to an old camp of Washington's above Bound-brook. Lieut.-Col. Simcoe's instructions were to burn these huts, if possible, in order to give as wide an alarm to the Jerseys as he could. He found it impracticable to do so, they not being joined in ranges nor built of very combustible materials. He proceeded without delay to Boundbrook, from whence he intended to carry off Col. Moyland, but he was not at Mr. Vanhorn's. Two officers who had been ill were there; their paroles were taken, and they were ordered to mark "Sick Quarters" over the room door they inhabited, which was done, and Mr. Vanhorn was informed that the party was the advanced guard of the left column of the army, which was commanded by General Birch, who meant to quarter that night at his house, and that Sir H. Clinton was in full march to Morristown with the army.

The party proceeded to Van-Vacter's bridge. Lieut.-Col. Simcoe found eighteen new flat-boats on carriages; they were full of water. He was determined effectually to destroy them. Combustibles had been applied for, and he had received in consequence a few port-fires. Every Hussar had a hand-grenade, and several hatchets were brought with the party. The timbers of the boats were cut through; they were filled with straw and railings, and some grenades being fastened in them, they were set on fire ; forty minutes were employed in this business. The country began to assemble in the rear, and as Lieut.-Col. Simcoe went to the Dutch meeting-house, where the harness and some stores were reported to be, a rifle-shot was fired at him from the opposite bank of the river. This house, with a magazine of forage, was now consumed, the commissary and his people being made prisoners.

The party proceeded to Somerset Court House, or Hillsborough. Lieut.-Col. Simcoe told the prisoners not to be alarmed, that he would give them their paroles before he left the Jerseys, but he could not help lamenting to the officers who were with him the sinister events which prevented him from being at Van-Vacter's bridge some hours sooner, as it would have been very feasible to have drawn off the flat-boats to the South River instead of destroying them.

At Somerset Court-House, three Loyalists who were prisoners there were liberated. One of them was a dreadful spectacle, he appeared to have been almost starved, and was chained to the floor. The soldiers wished, and were permitted to burn the Court-House. It was unconnected with any other building. By its flames it was shown on which side of the Rariton he was, and they would, most probably, alarm the neighbourhood of Brunswick, who would assemble at its bridge, to prevent him from returning by that road. The party proceeded towards Brunswick. Alarm guns were now heard, and some shots were fired in the rear, particularly by one person, who, as it afterwards appeared, being out a-shooting, and hearing of the incursion, had sent word to Governor Livingston, who was at Brunswick, that he would follow the party at a distance, and every now and then give a shot, that he might know which way they directed their march. Passing by some houses, Lieut.-Col. Simcoe told the women to inform four or five people, who were pursuing the rear, "that if they fired another shot, he would burn every house which he passed." A man or two were now slightly wounded. As the party approached Brunswick, Lieut.-Col. Simcoe began to be anxious for the cross-road, diverging from it into the Princetown road, which he meant to pursue, and of which, being once arrived at, he himself knew the by-ways he wished to attain, as he had frequently done duty there, and was minutely acquainted with every advantage and circumstance of the ground. His guide was perfectly satisfied that he had not yet arrived at this road; and Simcoe was in earnest conversation with him, and making the necessary enquiries, when a shot, at some little distance, discovered there was a party in the front. He immediately galloped forward and sent back Wright, his Orderly Sergeant to acquaint Captain Sandford, "that the shot had not been fired at the party," when, on the right, at some distance, he saw the rail fence (which was very high on both sides of the narrow road between two woods) somewhat broken down, and a man or two near it. Putting his horse to a canter, he joined the advance men of the Hussars, determining to pass through this opening so as to avoid every ambuscade that might be laid for him, or attack upon more equal terms Colonel Lee, whom he understood to be in the neighbourhood, and apprehended might be opposed to him, or any other enemy. Presently he saw some men concealed behind logs and bushes, between him and the opening he meant to pass through, and he heard the shout, "Now! now!" and found himself, when he recovered his senses, prisoner with the enemy, his horse having been killed under him with five bullets and himself, though unwounded, stunned by the violence of his fall.

The expedition was thus only partially successful; it would doubtless have succeeded had not the larger number of the boats been removed before the arrival of the Lieut.-Col. and his band at Van-Vacter's bridge. The Americans in the capture of Lieut.-Col. Simcoe became possessed of a rich prize, which they took care to keep behind bars till the last day of December, 1779. It was perhaps fortunate that the

Colonel on falling from his horse was stunned and rendered unconscious, as while he laid senseless on the ground Marener prevented a boy bayonetting him, saying, " Let him alone ; the rascal is dead enough ; " and another of the enemy regretted that he had not shot him through the head, which he would have done had he known him to be a Colonel ; but he thought " all Colonels wore lace."

Some little time after the accident befel Col. Simcoe there were some casualties which impeded the expedition. For example, when the British troops quitted the ranks at Hillsborough and marched to Brunswick several houses were burnt ; among others was the one which the guard relied upon as marking the private road a party of the Rangers was to take, and had been fixed upon as one of his guide-posts, as it were. Col. Simcoe, then at the head of the party, did not know of its being burnt, and by the destruction of the house he was led into an ambuscade. When the party had passed by on the full gallop they found themselves on the high land beyond the barracks at Brunswick. Here they rallied and had little doubt but that Lieut.-Col. Simcoe had been killed. The surgeon of the corps, with a white handkerchief held out as a flag of truce, at the manifest risk of his life, returned to enquire after him. The militia assembling, Captain Sandford drew up and charged them, when they fled. A Captain Voorhees, of the Jersey Continental troops, was overtaken, and a Hussar, at whom he had fired, killed him. This killing of Captain Voorhees was well-nigh being of the most serious consequence to Lieut.-Col. Simcoe. The populace of the country were incensed, indeed driven to fury, at his death, and would, even though Lieut.-Col. Simcoe was a prisoner, have been willing to wreak their vengeance on him had not such a catastrophe been prevented by other counsels. Injury to the Lieut.-Col. was averted by the Governor of the State issuing an order directed to that end. The order was as follows :

"The Governor being informed that some people have a desire to abuse and insult Lieut.-Col. Simcoe, a British captive, and wounded in a skirmish that happened this day between our militia and the British horse : though the Governor is not inclined to believe a report so great a disgrace upon the people of this State as that of the least inclination of revenge against a wounded enemy in our power; yet, to prevent the execution of any such attempt, it is his express order to treat the said officer according to the rules of war known and practised among all civilized nations ; and as it is his desire to be carried to Brunswick, it is his further orders that no molestation be given to him in his being carried hither, and that while there he be treated with that humanity which the United States of America have always observed towards their prisoners.

"WILLIAM LIVINGSTON.
"BRUNSWICK LANDING,
    "2nd October, 1779."

The following letter which Lieut.-Col. Simcoe received from Lieutenant J. Wilson, and preserved among his papers, shews the estimation in which he was held both by officers and men :

"RICHMOND, October 28, 1779.

"Yesterday and the part of the day before there was nothing but the picture of distress in every countenance ; but this morning the soldiers are shouting 'the father of the Rangers is alive' ; in short, nothing can exceed the joy which appears in the countenance of officers and soldiers, and prayers for your speedy recovery ; but none can possibly be more sincere than those of, etc.,

"J. WILSON."

On the day of the date of the above letter Simcoe was removed from Brunswick to Borden Town to a tavern kept by Col. Hoogland, of the Jersey Militia, by whom he was treated with great civility.   While there

Col. Lee, of the American service, who ever had the highest regard for Col. Simcoe and by his actions shewed he was anxious to be his friend, wrote offering him pecuniary assistance, which offer Simcoe was obliged to decline, as Lieut.-Col. Campbell, of the 74th Regiment, who was on parole, had kindly ministered to all his wants.

On the 5th November, 1779, Lieut.-Col. Simcoe received the following letter from Col. Lee :

" MONMOUTH, 6th Nov., 1779.

"SIR,—I am happy to learn by your polite reply, to an offer dictated by the feelings of man for man, that you had already been supplied in cash by the friendship of a brother officer ; should you hereafter stand in need of that article you will not suffer your want to continue long.   From some insinuations I have heard, and from a paragraph in the last Trenton *Gazette,* I apprehend your. local situation is not the most agreeable ; perhaps you may wish a remove, of course you must address the Governor, being employed in a similar line by our respective Generals ; it may not be amiss to appeal to me should His Excellency require contradiction to the reports propagated prejudicial to your character.   I am a stranger to what officer the barbarities on some captured militia in Buck's County,

Pennsylvania, can be truly attributed. I have never heard yourself declared as the author and am led to believe you were not present ; the unhappy sacrifice of Captain Voorhees in the late enterprise, I am told, took place after you fell. Your treatment of one of my dragoons, who fell into your hands last campaign, was truly generous ; and this made an impression on my mind which it still retains. Anxious to prevent injustice being done to the unfortunate I have been particular in the letter, though I please myself in presuming that it will be unnecessary.

" Your most immediate humble servant,

." H. LEE, Jun."

Lieut.-Col. Simcoe, in his reply, made his acknowledgments to Col. Lee, and informed him that no cruelties whatever were committed by the Queen's Rangers. On the 7th November Governor Livingston came to Bordentown. From what occurred in his conversation with him the Colonel had hopes of immediate exchange ; instead of this, however, he was removed to Burlington Jail. Col. Lee still continued his generous attention, and with persistent kindness supported the request which Lieut.-Col. Simcoe had made to be permitted to go on parole to Staten Island.

On November 14th Col. Lee wrote to Col. Simcoe as follows :

"Sir,—I have received an answer from Governor Livingston to my letter of request in your behalf, and although I cannot congratulate myself on its full success, I flatter myself it will lead to the completion of your wishes. The following is an extract from the Governor's letter :—'Col. Simcoe's treatment by this State is not founded on his character. We think it our indispensable duty to retaliate the enemy's severity to some of our citizens in New York ; but that such treatment should, however, happen to be exercised on a person of whom you entertain so favourable an opinion (besides the disagreeableness of such measure at any time,) is particularly afflictive to, etc., etc.' From the above declaration, I presume that your parole may be procured in a few days, if any expectation can be held out to the executive power of the State tending to a liberation of any of our citizens in New York. Perhaps your presence with Sir Henry Clinton might effect an alteration in the measures complained of, and a system of perfect liberality might be established in the future. If you will permit me to declare your determination on this point, and it answers my expectation, I will do myself the pleasure of waiting on the Governor in person to attempt the full settlement of the unhappy business.   I have as yet no reply from Mr. Boudinot, though his station does·not promise much service, and therefore his opinion will be very unimportant.

"I have the honour to be, etc.,

"H. LEE, Jr."

The letters which passed between Lieut.-Col. Simcoe and Col. H. Lee show that these officers were personally on the most friendly terms; each was willing to help the other in an emergency, while at the same time fulfilling all the requirements of military duty.   A great difficulty seems to have arisen in regard to the law and custom of exchange of prisoners.   Lieut.-Col. Simcoe was not disposed to submit to any indignity, nor was he in fear of any at the hand of Col. Lee, but he was not so confident in regard to other officials in the American service.   By a letter of Governor Livingston, addressed to Lieut.-Col. Simcoe in answer to a letter received from the Colonel without date, he expresses to him his wish that an exchange might take place, at the same time reminding him that his confinement was in consequence of the advice of the Privy Council, with which he could not interfere.   Later on Lieut.-Col. Simcoe enclosed the correspondence he had had with Governor Livingston, with a full statement of his case, to Sir Henry Clinton. The following is his letter to Sir Henry Clinton :—

"SIR,—Governor Livingston having promised me to forward to your Excellency my letters, I take the earliest opportunity of acquainting you with my late and present situation. The result of my incursion your Excellency is acquainted with, and I have only to observe that it was neither the valour of my enemies nor the least inattention of my party that occasioned my being made a prisoner, but it is to be attributed to the most common and malicious fortune. My life was preserved by the eagerness with which, as I have been informed, I was plundered when in a state of insensibility, and afterwards by the humanity of Mr. Morris. A Captain Voorhees was killed by the detachment in its return after I was taken ; his relations seemed to the Governor so determined to revenge his death by my destruction that he gave me a written protection, and afterwards directed Major Nairns, who treated me with great humanity, personally to prevent any injuries that might be offered to me. I was removed to Bordentown on my parole until the 9th, when I was taken from it and closely confined in Burlington Jail. As my commitment expressed no reason for this treatment, I wrote to Governor Livingston on the subject, and enclose to your Excellency the correspondence. I look upon my present situation as most particularly unfortunate. My private affairs called for my greatest attention, and having procured your Excellency's leave, I had great prospect of success in them.

"I trust, sir, that having obtained your recommendation near a twelvemonth since for promotion, you will still patronize the application you then honoured with your approbation. My fair fame has been struck at, and cruelty, the attribute of fear, has been imputed to me in the public prints and industriously propagated by ignorant, designing and cowardly people. My honest ambition has been most severely disappointed, and I am doomed to pass the flower of my youth in a gaol with criminals, when my state of health, affected by my fall, leads to an imbecility of mind that will not permit to me the consolations resulting from my liberal education. Yet, should I even be doomed obscurely to perish in the quicksand of deceit and calumny with which I am now surrounded, it is my duty to expect that no further ungenerous advantage may be permitted to the adversary who, trampling on the respect due to his own adherents, and presuming on the attention your Excellency may be inclined to pay to my situation, may think to offer without impunity some further insult to the British service, the liberal customs of war, and to the honour of my country.

"Of my proposed exchange, you, sir, are the best judge. Governor Livingston observed to me that I was the more likely to be immediately exchanged by being a prisoner of the State of New Jersey than if I had been taken by the Continental army. I acquiesced in his opinion, not then conceiving how much the field officers fighting under the banners of the State are depreciated in its estimation.

"There is one hope near, very near, to my heart, which is that your Excellency will promise my corps, and employ it in the same line as if I were present; its reputation would be the greatest comfort I could receive in a situation that excludes me from participating in its danger and its glory.   .   .   .   .   .   .

"Your most obedient and humble servant,

"J. G. SIMCOE."

This letter shows the constant care the Colonel had for his regiment, thinking more cf them than his own personal convenience, always, however, claiming to be treated as a prisoner of war and not as a common criminal; moreover, he would not submit to be exchanged for a number of privates of the enemy. In a letter to Governor Livingston he says:—"I do conceive, sir, that when it was proposed that Col.

Billop and I should be exchanged for Lieut.-Col. Reynolds and as many privates as make up the difference of rank between a Colonel and a private sentinel, that neither did you or the Council seriously imagine it could be accepted of. I know of no officer in the British army who, consistent with his duty, could apply or wish for so disproportionate a mode of exchange ; the proposal is ungenerous to your prisoners, nor do I conceive that your own field officers, or those whom you rank equal with them, will consider it as intended to expedite their return from captivity."

The state of affairs became so irksome to the Lieutenant-Colonel, and his treatment so contrary to what he conceived to be the rules of war in an honourable service, that he finally made an appeal direct to General Washington, and as that appeal obtained his release, I give his letter to General Washington, giving a history of his imprisonment and the efforts he had made for exchange or release. These efforts had hitherto been futile, and for causes which he could not or would not believe were known to the General commanding the American forces. His letter to General Washington was as follows :

Sir,—I am induced to lay myself before you from what I conceive to be a principle of duty, and that not merely personal. You may perhaps have heard, sir, of the uncommon fortune that threw me into the hands of the Jersey Militia. Governor Livingston told me I was a prisoner of state, a distinction I never till then was acquainted with, and observed that it was probable I should be soon exchanged as such, naming to me officers of similar rank as the likely persons.

" I was allowed my parole, was taken from it on the 9th, and have ever since been confined a close prisoner in Burlington, with Col. Billop, who is in irons and chained to the floor, to retaliate for F. Randolph and Leshier, the latter of whom is said to be confined in the same manner in New York. My *mittimus* hath not expressed what I am imprisoned for, but by the tenor of Governor Livingston's letters I suppose it is to retaliate for the former of those citizens, whom he allows to be a private soldier, and who is simply con⁻ fined as such.

" I apply to you, sir, either as a prisoner of war or as appealing to you from an unjustifiable stretch of power, without precedent or generosity. I am led to consider myself as a prisoner of war under your authority, from Governor Livingston's doubts expressed to me of his having the disposal of me ; from his correspondence with Gen. Robertson, published in the newspapers, where he submits Gen. Dickinson's prisoners to your disposal, and from Col. Billop, my fellow-prisoner, being taken by a party of Continental troops, receiving his parole from Mr. Beaty, and living under it till he was taken from it by a party of militia, and by Mr. Boudinot's orders confined in Burlington jail.

"He claims the protection that was first extended to him by the first Continental Commissary of prisoners.

"I hope, sir, you will make use of the power that I conceive enabled you to transfer Col. Billop to the State of New Jersey, in extending to me the rights allowed by civilized nations, and which, without a given reason, I have been deprived of.

"If, by any law I am acquainted with, I am in the power and disposal of Governor· Livingston, I think myself entitled to appeal to you, sir, from the injustice used toward me, as I cannot suppose there is no application for redress in a case which, if drawn into a precedent, must confound every distinction of rank, and will operate in a wider circle than that of the State of New Jersey.

"Governor Livingston has offered, as he has written to me, to exchange me for Lieut.-Col. Reynolds and Col. Billop for as many privates as made up his rank, naming among them the people for whom Col. Billop is avowedly retaliating. This proposition, I conceive, it never was supposed General Sir Henry Clinton could comply with.

" I hope, sir, you will do me the favour of early attending to this letter ; if Col. Billop only should be claimed by those whose prisoner he unquestionably appears to be, I should look upon it as a fortunate event, though I should be doomed to wear his ignominious chains.

" I am your obedient and humble servant,

"J. G. SIMCOE."

General Washington never answered this letter, but in a very few days Colonels Billop and Simcoe were exchanged. The exchange being effected on the last day of December, Lieut.-Col. Simcoe returned to Staten Island. He was mortified to find that the expedition, which was continued under the Commander-in-Chief, after his being taken prisoner, had failed. Upon his landing at Staten Island he received a letter from Major André, Adjutant-General, saying :—" If this meets you a free man prepare your regiment for embarkation, and hasten to New York yourself."

He immediately joined his corps at Richmond. Thus ended the campaign of 1779.

CHAPTER IV.

CAMPAIGN OF 1780.

E are now in 1780—the Queen's Rangers stationed on Staten Island, Richmond, at about the centre of the Island, being the head-quarters of the regiment. Major Armstrong, before the arrival of Lieut.-Col. Simcoe, had well fortified the place. By the 10th of January the communication between Staten Island and New York was totally shut off by floating ice. The Sound, which divides Staten Island from the Jerseys, was completely frozen over, and the ice was thick, and strong enough to bear cannon. Information was received that several. of the rebel Generals had been openly measuring the thickness of the ice, and it was universally rumoured that the Continentals were soon to make an attack on Staten Island. On the 15th January, early in the morning, the rebel detachment of nearly three thousand men, under the command of a person styled Lord Stirling, crossed on the ice and entered Staten Island.

Lord Stirling marched immediately towards the landing-place, and by his position cut off the British General's communication with the Volunteers of Ireland and the Queen's Rangers. Lieut.-Col. Simcoe occupied the high ground near Richmond, (Staten Island,) with small parties of cavalry, while the infantry were sedulously employed in strengthening the post. Lieut.-Col. Simcoe had every reason to believe that the post would be attacked by the American force which had landed on the Island, and had made every preparation for the defence of Richmond. To his surprise many deserters came in from the rebel army, and through them a perfect knowledge of the enemy's force was gained. One of them affirmed that he overheard some of their principal officers say " that it was not worth while to attack Richmond, where they were sure of obstinate resistance, and which must fall of itself whenever the main body was taken."

Lieut.-Col. Simcoe, knowing that the enemy had much the superior force, and that if an attack were made the post might be captured, had determined never to surrender himself or his force, but that, if driven to straits, the Queen's Rangers would disband, individually make their way from the island, and join the army stationed in Carolina. When Simcoe learned that the enemy had abandoned the idea of making an attack and were retreating from the island, he immediately pursued them with the flank companies and Hussars, and was overtaken by an order from General Stirling to effect the same purpose ; but the enemy had passed to the Jersey shore before he could come up with them.

The frost still continuing, there were many reports and a general expectation that the enemy would again adventure upon the island, with superior force and sufficient provision to attempt some greater purpose than the previous abortive effort to surprise the British troops, and at least to capture Richmond, and patrols were constantly made of all the roads by which they could possibly approach.

The Queen's Rangers had formerly experienced how ready General Stirling, in command on Staten Island, was to represent their services favourably, and they now, in common with the other troops, had a further proof of his inclinations in the general orders of the 21st January, when it was stated that, " Brigadier-General Stirling is happy to inform the troops on this island of His Excellency General Kniphausen's fullest approbation of their behaviour, and the good countenance they showed when the rebels were upon this island, which the Brigadier had reported to the Commander-in-Chief ; and His Excellency desires his thanks may be given to them."

On the 25th January Lieut.-Col. Simcoe gave out the following order, " That he expects the order relative to officers and soldiers sleeping in their clothes be strictly complied with, such recruits excepted whom the officers commanding companies may judge as yet unequal to the duties of the regiment ; if any half-bred soldier disobeys this order, the first officer, or non-commissioned officer, who meets with him will deliver him to the officer on guard, to be put on some internal duty. The Lieut.-Col. has particular satisfaction in seeing the General's approbation of that good countenance which enabled him, on the late inroad of the enemy, to rest perfectly at ease, without augmenting the duty of the regiment ; he knows its universal spirit, and, certain of the fidelity of those on guard, that the garrison cannot be snatched away by surprise, is confident that Richmond redoubts will be too dear for the whole rebel army to purchase."

Soon after the rebel army returned to their former winter quarters, Colonel Simcoe got intelligence that General Washington was quartered at a considerable distance from his army, or any corps of it, and nearer to New York. This intelligence induced Lieut.-Col. Simcoe to undertake a bold and dashing venture, which was no other than to surprise General Washington, capture and hold him as a prisoner of war. Simcoe made all preparation to carry out this enterprise and felt certain of success, when he learned that Captain Beckwith, General Kniphausen's

Aide-de-Camp, had also formed a plan to carry off General Washington. The result was that Lieut.-Col. Simcoe had to give up his undertaking and give aid to Captain Beckwith, who obtained the Hussars of the Queen's Rangers to assist him. Captain Beckwith, with a body of men, attempted to carry out his purpose, but, owing to an alarm being given, his men and those of the enemy got into a conflict. A number were killed or wounded on both sides ; the undertaking proved a failure, General Washington was not captured, and the Hussars returned to Staten Island.

The ice floating on the 22nd February, the Sound became impassable, and the soldiers were permitted to undress themselves at night ; and in case of alarm they were directed to accoutre in their shirts, and to form at their posts.

On the 21st of April of this year, 1780, we find the Queen's Rangers at Charlestown, South Carolina, which was being besieged by the southern force of the British army. The camping-ground of the Rangers was at the Quarter House, five miles from Charlestown.

When Lieut.-Col. Simcoe was at Charlestown the Commander-in-Chief showed him a letter which he had just received from the Colonial Secretary, written under the impression that the Lieut.-Col. had been killed in the fall from his horse, as had been reported. In this letter was a .paragraph which was a tribute to Lieut.-Col. Simcoe's worth and the estimation in which he was held by the Home Government. The paragraph was as follows :—" The loss of so able and gallant an officer as Colonel Simcoe is much to be lamented, but I hope his misfortune will not damp the spirit of the brave Loyalists he so often led out unto success. His last enterprise was certainly a very bold one, and I should be glad he had been in a situation to be informed that his spirited conduct was approved of by the King."

Nothing gratified Lieut.-Col. Simcoe so much as the good repute of his regiment. When he arrived at Charlestown he was warmly welcomed by his friends after his long and severe imprisonment. To these warm congratulations of his friends he referred in orders, saying that he had great pleasure " in hearing the uniformity and appearance of the regiment universally approved ; he trusts that soldier will vie with soldier and officer with officer in maintaining in their respective stations the very favourable impression which their superior officers entertain of them, that their discipline and appearance on the parade reflects credit on their soldier-like behaviour in the field."

The Queen's Rangers, on their arrival before Charlestown, were four hundred, rank and file, and proved a valuable accession to the troops besieging Charlestown. The siege was pushed with vigour, and on the 12th of May the British force had the satisfaction of congratulating themselves on the fact that the Americans on that day capitulated and surrendered the place. After the surrender of Charlestown the regiment advanced to Four-hole Bridge, where they remained a day or two at Caton's (an unfortunate Loyalist whom the rebels assassinated), from whence by express order they returned to Charlestown, as it was supposed to embark on an expedition to Georgetown. They reached the head-quarters on the 30th of May and embarked on the 31st for New York.

On the 21st June the regiment landed at Staten Island and marched to Richmond redoubts, the camping-ground of the previous winter. At midnight Lieut.-Colonel Simcoe received orders to proceed instantly to the Jerseys. On the 23rd June Major-General Matthews, with a division of the troops, marched before day for Springfield ; the Rangers formed the advanced guard. On the march to Springfield a good deal of skirmishing took place and some fighting. The enemy retreated, and Colonel Simcoe and the Rangers arrived at Springfield with the loss of but a few men. On this expedition into the Jerseys, the Jersey Continental Militia suffered severely under an artillery attack, and among others, Fitz-Randolph, one of their best officers, was killed. At night the troops, having harassed the enemy considerably, retired over the bridge of boats which had been made between Staten Island and Jersey to Staten Island, the retreat being covered by two redoubts, occupied by troops of the line, who embarked, on the bridge being broken up, without molestation. This retreat was ordered by the Commander-in-Chief. He, having had information that a French armament was about to make an appearance at Rhode Island, was anxious that Kniphausen's brigade should be ready to attack it on its arrival. He had encamped the army near Kingsbridge, ready for an attack, and pursuant to orders the Rangers embarked the next morning, and sailing up the North River, landed on the 25th, and took up their position in front of the line. Between the 25th June and 19th July Lieut.-Col. Simcoe was indisposed, and was obliged to go to New York to recover his health. On the 19th July he rejoined his corps, and proceeded with it to Long Island.

Lieut.-Col. Simcoe burned with desire to meet an armament of Frenchmen, to whom he owed a deadly hostility, on account, it may be, of his father having met his death while engaged in the King's service upon the important expedition against Quebec in 1759. Through Major André he communicated his wishes, and his hope, to the Commander-in-Chief that in case of any attack on Rhode Island he would employ the Rangers in it. Major André replied : " The General assures you that the Rangers shall be pitted against a

French regiment the first time he can procure a meeting."

On the 25th August the Commander-in-Chief augmented the Rangers with two troops of dragoons, appointed Lieut.-Col. Simcoe to be Lieut.-Col. of Cavalry, and the infantry captains, Saunders and Shank, officers of distinguished merit, to the additional troops. The corps remained at Oyster Bay, Long Island, until the 22nd September, when it marched to Jamaica, Long Island.

We have now reached a period in the campaigns of 1780 when an event occurred which cast a gloom over the whole army. This was the arrest, imprisonment, and subsequent execution as a spy of Major André, who was a special friend of Lieut.-Col. Simcoe, and Adjutant-General of the British forces. At this time the Americans had in their service an officer of rank, whose name has become a synonym for treason, on account of his perfidy in the service he had espoused. Benedict Arnold was a man of a headstrong nature, fond of show, greedy for money that would enable him to exercise his ostentation, and withal unscrupulous. On the breaking out of the Revolution he kept a drug store at New Haven, in Connecticut. Being in command of a volunteer company there, when the war broke out, he marched to Cambridge, and thence his career is identified with some of the bravest exploits of the Revolution,

MAJOR ANDRE.

From a pen-and-ink drawing taken by himself the day before his Execution.

until his defection and disgrace in 1780. When the British evacuated Philadelphia in the spring of 1778, Arnold was appointed by Washington Military Governor of the city, having in command a small detachment of troops. Fond of show and inflated with the importance of his station, he lived in a style of splendour and extravagance which his income would not allow, and so became pecuniarily embarrassed. In Philadelphia he resided in the spacious mansion that once belonged to William Penn, Governor of Pennsylvania, and eclipsed all others in the capital of Pennsylvania in his luxurious style of living. Rather than retrench expenses and live within his means, he chose to procure money by a system of fraud and prostitution of his official power, which brought him into collision with the people and with the President and Council of Pennsylvania. The latter preferred a series of charges against him, all implying a wilful abuse of power and criminal acts. These charges were submitted to a joint committee of Congress and the Assembly and Council of Pennsylvania. After proceeding in their duties for a while, it was thought expedient to hand the whole matter over to General Washington, and the charges were transmitted to him. The military trial commenced on the 20th December, 1779, and continued, with slight interruptions, until the 26th January, 1780, when the verdict was rendered. Arnold was acquitted of two of the four charges, the other two were sustained in part. He had expected from the court a triumphant vindication of his character and was, or pretended to be, incensed at not getting a full acquittal.

He is said by one historian of the times " to have made an elaborate defence, in the course of which he magnified his services, asserted his entire innocence of the charges made against him, cast reproach by imputation upon some of the purest men in the army, and solemnly proclaimed his patriotic attachment to his country."

Another historian (Sparks) says : " The boastfulness and malignity of these declarations are obvious enough ; but their consummate hypocrisy can be understood only by knowing the fact that at the moment they were uttered he had been eight months in secret correspondence with the enemy, and was prepared, if not resolved, when the first opportunity should offer to desert and destroy his country."

By dint of much persevering solicitation, he had succeeded in persuading General Washington to give him the command of West Point, on the Hudson. General Washington had no suspicion that he had been plotting treason with the enemy and no doubt appointed him to this post, (which he did on the 3rd August, 1780,) owing to the show of patriotism which he made, and to the anxious desire he expressed to serve, and if necessary to die for his bleeding country. Having secured the command of West Point, Arnold was afforded abundant opportunity of carrying out his project of betraying those who had placed faith in his integrity. Sir Henry Clinton, the British Commander, was not unwilling to accept the surrender of a .post, which he of course considered rightly belonged to the British, though temporarily held by Colonists in treasonable rebellion against the British crown. Whether or not Sir Henry Clinton believed that Arnold was actuated by a patriotic desire to return to his old love and renew his allegiance to the Crown, or whether he knew that Arnold was acting from a merely sordid motive, or to gratify his revenge for wrong, or fancied wrong, is not very clear. The negotiations for the surrender of West Point were carried on by Major André, under the fictitious name of John Anderson, on behalf of the British and by Arnold himself on his own behalf, but under the fictitious name of Gustavus. Writing in a disguised hand, he clothed his meaning in the ambiguous style of a commercial correspondence.

André at the time was Aide-de-Camp of the Commander-in-Chief. He enjoyed his unbounded confidence, and to him, when the name and station of Arnold became known, was entrusted the delicate task of consummating the bargain with Arnold.

The general plan for placing West Point in the hands of the British was well conceived, and had it not been that Major André unwittingly allowed himself to be inveigled within the American lines, would most likely have succeeded. Whether it succeeded or not, Major André, who was as honourable as he was gallant, it is more than probable, would not have been made a victim of the treachery and rapacity of Benedict Arnold.

In negotiating the terms of surrender Arnold had arranged that Major André was to proceed in the *Vulture* down the Hudson opposite a point about four miles from the house of one Smith. Smith was to take André from the *Vulture,* land him at the foot of a hill, called Long Clove Mountain, on the western shore of the Hudson, about two miles below a place called Haverstraw. This place had been designated by Arnold for the place of meeting, and thither he had repaired from Smith's house. This project was carried out. Arnold was concealed in the thick bushes, and to the same place Smith conducted André. They were left alone, and for the first time heard each other's voice. There, in the gloom of night, the negotiation was entered upon, pursued, and when dawn approached the conference was still in progress. Smith, who was not present at the conference, came and warned them of the necessity for haste. There was much to do, and

André reluctantly consented to mount the horse ridden by Arnold's servant and accompany Arnold to Smith's house, nearly four miles distant. It was yet,dark, and the voice of a sentinel, near the village of Haverstraw, gave André the first intimation that he was within the American lines. He felt his danger, but it was too late to recede. His uniform was effectually concealed by a long blue surtout, yet the real danger that surrounded him, (he being within the enemy's line without a pass or flag,) made him exceedingly uneasy. They arrived at Smith's house at dawn, and at that moment they heard a cannonade in the direction of the *Vulture.* The American Commander, Col. Livingston, had been informed that the vessel lay so near the shore as to 'be within cannon-shot. Accordingly, in pursuance of his order, the Americans opened fire upon the *Vulture* with such severity that she hoisted her anchor and dropped farther down the river. This movement André beheld with anxiety. Here he was, within the American lines, with no apparent means of escape. As far as he was concerned, he was engaged in a lawful enterprise, was acting under the orders of his commanding officer in the negotiation for the surrender. He made a fatal mistake, however, when he passed American lines. The orders of Sir Henry Clinton were that the negotiation with Arnold was not to take place within the American lines, but on neutral territory. It was entirely owing to the deception practised on Major André by Arnold, that André was found outside of the ground occupied by the British troops. Lossing, in his " Field Book of the American Revolution," after describing the incidents connected with the conference at Smith's house within the American lines, has appended this note :—" The fact that Arnold had provided a spare horse is evidence that he expected a longer conference than the remainder of the night would afford. Furthermore, convicted as Arnold is of innate wickedness, it may not be unjust to suppose that he was prepared, after getting André within the American lines, to perform any act of dishonour to extort a high price for his treason, or to shield himself from harm if circumstances should demand it."

There is much reason in what the writer has said : for three weeks previous to this he wrote André in the feigned hand and style to which I have before alluded, and said, referring to himself in the third person. "He (*i.e.*, Arnold) is still of opinion that his first purpose is by no means unreasonable, and makes no doubt when he has a conference with you, that you will close with it. He expects, when you meet, that you will be fully authorized from your house ; that the rules and profits of the co-partnership may be fully understood. *A speculation of this kind might be as easily made with ready money.*" Can anything be stronger to prove that Arnold, at all events, in his negotiation for the surrender of his post, and in his treachery to the American army and the American people, was actuated by a desire for money, or as Mr. Lossing, already referred to, has expressed it: " Money was the grand lure that made Arnold a traitor."

The plot for the surrender, there is no doubt, was fully consummated at the conference between Major André and Arnold, on the night and morning of the 21st and 22nd September, 1780, on the banks of the Hudson, at Clove Mountain, and the details were completed ready for execution at the house of Joshua Hett Smith.

All the plans for the surrender of West Point, and the manner in which it was to be effected being arranged, Arnold supplied André with papers explanatory of the military condition of the garrison and its dependencies. These Arnold requested André to place between his stockings and feet, and in the event of accident to destroy them. He then gave him a pass, and bidding André adieu, went up the river in his own barge to headquarters, fully believing that no obstacle now interposed to frustrate his scheme. Major André determined to make his way the best he could to New York. He would have prepared to join the *Vulture* and gone by water, but Smith, on whom he relied to row him to the vessel, positively refused to go. Smith offered to ride half the night on horseback if he would take a land route. Having no other means of reaching the vessel, André was obliged to yield to the force of circumstances. He had been prevailed upon by Arnold to exchange his military coat for a citizen's dress—a fatal error. In his journey to New York he reached Tarrytown, a village on the eastern bank of the Hudson, twenty-seven miles from New York. He slept at Tarrytown that night, and after a frugal repast, continued his journey. It happened that a band of volunteers had been sent out to guard the roads leading from Tarrytown to New York, and to prevent cattle being driven to New York, and to arrest any suspicious characters who might travel that way. The band of volunteers, some of them meeting André, stopped him in his journey, ordered him to pull off his boots, found the papers which Arnold had told him to conceal between his boots and stockings, arrested him as a spy, and turned him over to the officer in command of the nearest military post. For a long time the volunteers who arrested André were called " Patriots ; " but the truth is they were in · no sense patriots, nor did they act from patriotic motives. From documentary evidence made public for the first time a few years ago, it has been made apparent that even after discovering the compromising papers on

André, they would have released him if he had had at his command and could have paid them at the time 500 or 1,000 guineas for his ransom; but, having neither the money or the means of giving security at once, he was delivered up to his fate. The papers found on André's person were sent to General Washington. Pursuant to an order from him André was conducted to West Point, where he remained until the morning of the 28th September, when he was conveyed to Stony Point, and thence conducted under a strong escort to Tappan on the Hudson. On the arrival of General Washington at Tappan, he ordered a Court of Inquiry. This Court, consisting of fourteen general officers, was convened at Tappan on the 29th September, and on that day Major André was arraigned before it and examined. André made a plain statement of the facts, acknowledged and confirmed the truthfulness of his statements in his letter to Washington from Salem; confessed that he came ashore from the *Vulture* in the night, and without a flag; answered the query of the Board whether he had anything further to say respecting the charges made against him by remarking, "I leave them to operate with the Board, persuaded you will do me justice." He was remanded to prison, and after a long deliberation the Board reported: "That Major André, Adjutant-General of the British Army, ought to be considered as a spy from an enemy, and that, agreeably to the law and usage of nations, it is their opinion that he ought to suffer death."

On the next day General Washington signified his approval of the decision as follows: "The Commander-in-Chief approves of the opinion of the Board of General Officers respecting Major André and orders that the execution of Major André take place to-morrow at five o'clock, p.m."

Lossing, the American writer to whom I have before referred, in his account of the unhappy matter has written : " The youth, candour and gentlemanly bearing of André during the trying scenes of his execution made a deep impression upon the Court ; and had the decision of those officers been in consonance with their feelings instead of their judgment and the stern necessities imposed by the expedients of war he would not have suffered death.   When the decision of the Court was made known to him the heroic firmness of his mind challenged the admiration of all.   He exhibited no fear of death, but the manner of his death was a subject that gave him uneasiness; he wished to die as a *soldier*, not as a *spy*.   Lossing goes on to say, " There could be no question among military men as to the equity of André's sentence, and yet there was a general desire on the part of the Americans to save his life.   Washington was deeply impressed with this feeling and was ready to employ any measure to effect it consistent with his public duty."

When Mr. Lossing says, "There could be no question among military men as to the equity of André's sentence," he is speaking for American military men ; that has never been the opinion entertained by British military men or by the British people generally. The sentence on Major André has been condemned by them and considered an injustice—a sentence contrary to all moral, civil and military law. Major André never should have been treated as a spy and compelled to suffer as such. It is true that nufortunately he met Arnold within the American lines, but he was not there of his own free will, but was betrayed into going there by Arnold. As already stated André was surprised when he found himself there. It was against the order of the Commander-in-Chief that he entered the enemy's lines and he did not know that he was there till it was too late to retire. The general opinion of Englishmen is that he ought to have been treated as a military prisoner, taken in lawful enterprise, and exchanged as a prisoner, not hanged as a spy, an end he so much abhorred· As to the changing of his clothes, when he found himself in the camp of the enemy, he did this on the suggestion of Arnold, who advised him to doff his military uniform and put on civilian's clothes. If the

London *General Evening Post* of November 14th, 1780, is to be credited, when being led to the scaffold to be executed as a spy, his last words were, "Remember that I die as a British officer, while the manner of my death must reflect disgrace on your commander."

Miss Seward, Major André's early friend, on reading the account in the London *General Evening Post* just quoted, wrote thus in her "Monody on Major André":

> Oh Washington! I thought thee great and good,
> Nor knew thy Nero-thirst for guiltless blood,
> Severe to use the power that Fortune gave,
> Thou cool, determined murderer of the brave!
> Lost to each fairer virtue that inspires
> The genuine fervour of the patriot fires!
> And you, the base abettors of the doom
> That sunk his blooming honours in the tomb,
> The opprobrious tomb your hardened hearts decreed
> While all he asked was as the brave to bleed!

Major André was a thorough soldier, and if in the fortunes of war his doom was sealed, all he asked and prayed for was that he might be shot, and so end his life in a soldier's death. To be treated as a spy, when he knew he was but doing his duty as a soldier, was abhorrent to his nature. The execution, although fixed for the 1st of October, did not actually take place till the 2nd October, 1780. On the morning of the day fixed for his execution he sketched with a pen a likeness of himself. Up to the day of his execution he was not without hope that an exchange would be effected. When being conveyed to the place of execution he suddenly came in view of the gallows, when he involuntarily started backward and made a pause. "Why this emotion, sir?" said an officer by his side. Instantly recovering his composure he said, "I am reconciled to my death, but I detest the mode." He seems to have been determined that never should an executioner perform the task of adjusting the rope to his neck, for when he reached the gallows, and the ghastly rope hung before him, he slipped the noose over his head and adjusted it himself; the waggon on which he stood was removed from under him, he was suspended and almost instantly expired. The American historian, quoting from *The Military Journal*, says: "He was dressed in his royal regimentals and boots. His remains, in the same dress, were placed in an ordinary coffin and interred at the foot of the gallows, and the spot was consecrated by the tears of thousands. Thus died, in the bloom of life, the accomplished Major André, the pride of the royal army and the valued friend of Sir Henry Clinton."

Though committed to the dust in America his remains were taken up in 1831 by Mr. Buchanan, the

British Consul at New York, removed to England, and deposited near his monument in Westminster Abbey.

Let us now see how Lieut.-Col. Simcoe viewed the taking off of his intimate friend Major André, and how he would have prevented it if he could.

Upon the first intimation of Major André's detention, Lieut.-Col. Simcoe by letter, desired Lieut.-Col. Crosbie to inform the Commander-in-Chief " that if there was any possibility of rescuing him, he and the Queen's Rangers were ready to attempt it, not doubting to succeed in whatever a similar force would effect." At the same time he sent out persons to watch the road between Washington's Camp and Philadelphia; for he reasoned that without the concurrence of Congress that general would not proceed to extremities, and that probably he would send Major André to Philadelphia, in which case he might possibly be retaken upon the road thither. Lieut.-Col. Simcoe wrote to Col. Lee, of whose generous temper he had personally received so many proofs, to procure an interview with him, ostensibly for the exchange of prisoners, but really to converse with him relative to Major André.

Col. Lee answered his letter on the 2nd October, the day of André's execution; stating his intention to attend to the release of certain prisoners, and added the following postscript, " Since writing the foregoing

I find that Sir Henry Clinton's offers have not come up to what was expected, and that this. hour is fixed for the execution of the sentence. How cold the friendship of those in power!"

This postscript plainly referred to André, and amounts to a distinct statement that Sir Henry Clinton had made offers for a release of André, but that these offers were not such as could be accepted.

Lieut.-Col. Simcoe in his answer said, " I am at a loss to express myself on the latter paragraph (postscript) of your letter ; I have long accustomed myself to be silent, or to speak the language of the heart. The useless murder of Major André, would almost, were it possible, annihilate that wish which, consentaneous to the ideas of our Sovereign and the Government of Great Britain, has ever operated on the officers of the British army—the wish of a reconciliation and speedy reunion with their revolted fellow-subjects in America.

" Sir Henry Clinton has the warmest feelings for those under his command, and was ready to have granted for Major André's exchange, whatever ought to have been asked.

" Though every desire that I had formed to think, in some instances, favourably of those who could urge, or of him who could permit, the murder of this most virtuous and accomplished gentleman, be now totally eradicated, I must still subscribe myself with great personal respect, sir,

" Your most obedient and obliged servant,

" J. G. SIMCOE."

Lieut.-Col. Simcoe, in the Appendix to his Military Journal, has stated that as a matter of fact Sir Henry Clinton did not make any offer to the American Commander for the delivering up or release of Major André. We may well regret this. Was it due to over punctiliousness, that an offer was not made for an officer in such imminent peril as Major André? Surely it would not have been unbecoming in the British Commander to have offered to exchange prisoners in his custody for André without waiting for an overture from the American Commander. I make this statement with all the modesty of a civilian not skilled in military tactics. Although Col. Lee stated that offers were made by Sir Henry Clinton, but that they had " not come up to what was expected," Lieut.-Col. Simcoe states the opposite in his own language, as follows :—" There were no offers whatsoever made by Sir Henry Clinton. Amongst some letters which passed on this unfortunate event, a paper was slid in without signature, but in the hand-writing of Hamilton, Washington's Secretary, saying, ' that the only way to save André was to give up Arnold.'" Lieut.-Col. Simcoe, still adhering to his opinion that Major André was murdered, thus proceeds :—"Major André was murdered upon private, not public, considerations. It bore not with it the stamp of justice, for there was not an officer in the British army whose duty it would not have been, had any of the American Generals offered to quit the service of Congress to have negotiated to receive them, so that this execution could not, by example, have prevented the repetition of the same offence.

"It may appear that from his change of dress, etc., he came under the description of a spy ; but when it shall be considered against his stipulation, intention and knowledge, he became absolutely a prisoner, and was forced to change his dress for self-preservation, it may safely be asserted that no European General would on this pretext have had his blood upon his head. He fell a sacrifice to that which was expedient, not to that which was just ; what was supposed to be useful superseded what would have been generous, and though by imprudently carrying papers about him he gave a colour to those who endeavoured to separate Great Britain from America to press for his death, yet an open and elevated mind would have found greater satisfaction in the obligations it might have laid on the army of his opponents, than in carrying into execution a useless and unnecessary vengeance.

" It has been said that not only the French party from their customary policy, but Mr. Washington's personal enemies urged him on, contrary to his inclinations, to render him unpopular if he executed Major André, or suspected if he pardoned him."

The officers and soldiers of the Queen's Rangers personally knew and highly esteemed Major André. Lieut.-Col. Simcoe, in order to evince their grief at his fate, and respect for his memory, took the opportunity in his orders to inform them that " he had given directions that the regiment should immediately be provided with black and white feathers as mourning for the late Major André, an officer whose superior integrity and uncommon ability did honour to his country and to human nature. The Queen's Rangers will never sully their glory in the field by an undue severity : they will, as they have ever done, consider those to be under their protection who shall be in their power, and will strike with reluctance at their unhappy fellow-subjects, who, by a system of the basest artifices, have been seduced from their allegiance and disciplined to revolt ; but it is the Lieutenant-Colonel's most ardent hope that, on the close of some decisive victory, it will be the regiment's fortune to secure the murderers of Major André, for the vengeance due to an injured nation and an insulted army."

With the orders superadded to the expression of

opinion of Lieut.-Col. Simcoe above given, I close my narrative of the circumstances under which a very gallant and noble officer of the British service was done to death. Much controversy has been had relative to his tragic end. He was a close and personal friend of Lieut.-Col. Simcoe, hence my desire to present the facts as he regarded them, at the same time embodying much of what an American historian has given on the same subject. At this date, looking back on the time and concurrent events, the favourable disposition and respect which the Americans had for Major André, it may be conjectured at least, that had not America been in alliance with France, and a foreign policy introduced in the case, the life of Major André might have been preserved to adorn the land of his birth and the profession of his adoption.

Lieut.-Col. Simcoe was a great favourite of the Loyalists of America, whose battles he was fighting. Soon after Major André's death the Loyalists of Pennsylvania gave him a paper begging him to forward to the Colonial Secretary, Lord St. Germain, their requisition which accompanied it : "That he, Lieut.-Col. Simcoe, might be detached with a thousand men to a certain place with arms, and that they, to the amount of some thousands, would instantly join and declare for Government;" it concluded with the strongest encomiums on the character of the officer whom they wished to command them, and of the confidence with which they would take up arms.

This communication was so personal to himself that the Lieutenant-Colonel informed the deputation that he could not, as a subordinate officer, forward it to Great Britain without the knowledge of the Commander-in-Chief. The requisition was afterwards put in a shape, which made it not imperative for him to show it to the Commander-in-Chief, and then, with his approbation, he made answer, in substance, thanking them for their confidence, and saying that " they could not but see that the system of the Commander-in-Chief was to unravel the thread of the rebellion from the southward; and that in its progress your most valuable assistance will be depended upon."

The campaign of 1780 is now coming to a close. On the 12th November we find Lieut.-Col. Simcoe at the post of Richmond, Staten Island. The French General La Fayette was in the neighbourhood of Elizabethtown, in force and with boats on travelling carriages. It was supposed that La Fayette meditated an attack on Richmond. Official information was sent by the Adjutant-General to Lieut.-Col. Simcoe that his post was the object of La Fayette's design, and that it would probably be attacked on the ensuing night ; he immediately declared in orders : " The Lieutenant-Colonel has received information that M. Fayette, a Frenchman, at the head of some of His Majesty's deluded subjects, has threatened to plant a French colony on Richmond redoubts. The Lieutenant-Colonel believes the report to be a gasconade; but as the evident ruin of the enemy's affairs may prompt them to some desperate attempt, the Queen's Rangers will lay in their clothes this night; and have their bayonets in perfect order."

The Highlanders immediately assembled and marched to the redoubts which, in the distribution of posts, was allotted them to defend, and displaying their national banner, with which they used to commemorate their Saint's day,. fixed it on the ramparts saying, " No Frenchman or rebel shall ever pull that down."

The rumoured attack proved to be only a false alarm, and the Rangers were permitted to pass the remainder of the year in comparative peace.

CHAPTER V.

Campaign of 1781.

THE Campaign of 1781 commenced with an expedition into Virginia under command of General Arnold. The Queen's Rangers formed a part of the force in this expedition, which sailed from Sandy Hook, reaching the point of their destination at Hood's Point, on James' River, on 3rd January. General Arnold ordered Lieut.-Col. Simcoe to land with one hundred and thirty of the Queen's Rangers, and the Light Infantry, and Grenadiers of the 80th Regiment. Shortly after landing the expedition was pushed on up the river to Westover, and thence on for Richmond, the intended point of attack. On the second day's march from Westover towards Richmond, some of the enemy's militia were met; they were deceived by the dress of the Queen's Rangers, and met with one of those military jokes on the part of Lieut.-Col. Simcoe which surprised the Continentals not a little. As the militia approached Lieut.-Col. Simcoe, they thought that the Rangers, dressed in green like themselves, were of their party.

Lieut.-Col. Simcoe reprimanded them for not coming sooner, held conversation with them, and then sent them prisoners to General Arnold. The word now came, "On to Richmond!" The command was obeyed; the heights in rear of the town were gained; then the lower town; the defenders were panic-stricken, fled from the place; were pursued several miles, and some of the enemy captured, besides horses, much wanted for the service. On Lieut.-Col. Simcoe's return, he met with orders from General Arnold to march to the foundry at Westham, six miles from Richmond, and to destroy it; this he accomplished, taking the powder stored in the magazine there and pouring it into the water. Soon after this, while the troops were halting at Westover, information was obtained that the enemy was assembled at the Charles City Court-House; an advance was made to surprise and attack the enemy at this point. The advance guard made a prisoner of one of the patrols met on the way, gained the enemy's countersign, which stood them in good stead in the prosecution of the enterprise, marched on and succeeded in their undertaking. The Continental Militia were at that place commanded by General Nelson, and consisted of seven or eight hundred men; they were completely frightened and dispersed. Serjeant Adams of the Queen's Rangers Hussars was mortally wounded in the attack on Charles City Court-

House.   This gallant soldier, sensible of his situation, said, " My beloved Colonel, I do not mind dying but for God's sake, do not leave me in the hands of the rebels."   Serjeant Adams died at Westover on the 9th January : the corps attended his funeral ; he was buried in the colours which had been displayed and taken from Hood's battery.   The British troops had much reason to know at this time that they were really in the enemies' country—there were enemies to the right of them, to the left of them, and in front of them.   The Rangers were on constant duty, ranging over the country feeling the enemy, skirmishing and attacking outposts.   Stratagem to capture the enemy was often resorted to.   General Arnold employed the garrison in fortifying the post at Portsmouth, the primary object of his expedition.   On the 29th January Lieut.-Col. Simcoe was sent to fortify the post at Great Bridge ; here the rebels continually fired at the Ranger sentries at night, which became very annoying ; the troops had much hard and fatiguing duty during the day, which demanded of them as much quiet as possible during the night ; this induced them to place decoy sentinels for the enemy to fire at instead of the real ones they supposed them.   A figure was dressed up with a blanket coat, and posted in the road by which the enemy would probably advance, and files resembling those of a piquet, were placed at the customary distance. At midnight the rebels arrived, and fired twenty or thirty shots at the effigy. As they ran across the road, they exposed themselves to the shots of two sentinels ; they then made off. The next day an officer happening to come in with a flag of truce, he was shown the figure, and was made sensible of the inhumanity of firing at a sentinel, when no further attack was intended. Lieut.-Col. Simcoe says in his journal, " This ridicule probably had a good effect, as during the stay of the Queen's Rangers at Great Bridge, no sentinel was fired at."

General Arnold on the 13th of February received information of the arrival of three French ships of the line. Captain Alberson, the gallant master of the *Empress of Russia*, Lieut.-Col. Simcoe's transport, was anxious and offered his services to lay him and the Queen's Rangers on board any of the French ships. Lieut.-Col. Simcoe, like many others, felt that without the assistance the French afforded to the Revolutionists the war would be brought to a speedy determination, Hence his wish at any and all times to engage in an attack on the French, the American allies.

The campaigning in Virginia still continued. The American Militia assembling at Hampton, Lieut -Col. Dundas passed over from Portsmouth to dislodge them. What part the Rangers bore in this expedition cannot be better detailed than in the modest recital of Quartermaster McGill, of the Queen's Rangers, who went with Col. Dundas, and whose bravery and conduct were honoured with high commendations by that most respectable officer: "Col. Dundas, with part of his regiment, a few Yagers, Lieut. Holland, myself (McGill) and twelve Hussars of the Queen's Rangers went on an expedition towards Hampton. We embarked on the night of the 6th. of March, and landed early next morning at Newport ; next from thence marched to a village about three miles from Hampton, where we destroyed some stores and burned four large canoes without opposition ; but on our return to the boats we saw about two hundred militia drawn up on a plain and a wet ditch in front. As I was advanced with the Hussars and first saw them, I informed the Colonel and at the same time asked his permission to advance against them, without thinking of Lieut. Holland, whom, in truth, I did not see at the time. He granted my request and ordered the mounted men of the 8oth to join me, who had, as well as the Rangers, been mounted in the morning upon the march. With these and some officers of the 8oth, who also got horses, we made up twenty-six horsemen. The rebels were about three hundred yards from the road, and I had to wheel to the left full in their view, which discovered our numbers and, I believe, encouraged them a good deal, as they did not fire till we were within thirty yards of

them. This checked us and gave them time to give us a second salute, but not with the same effect, for with the first they killed Captain Stewart, of the 80th ; wounded Lieut. Salisbury, of the navy, who commanded the boats and came for pleasure ; Col. Dundas, myself, and Sergeant Galloway were unhorsed, and some of the infantry who were a hundred yards in our rear were wounded. My horse had three balls through him, and he received a fourth before all was over.   .   .   .
The rebels had sixty killed, wounded and taken ; among the latter was their commander, Col. Curl, and a few of their officers. I cannot ascertain our loss more than I have mentioned. They let us embark quietly, and we landed at Portsmouth the same evening." The McGill who made this report was that John McGill who has been mentioned in Scadding's work, "Toronto of Old," page 260 : " In the number of the *Gazette* for May, 1793, we have ten guineas reward offered for the recovery of a government grindstone ; ten guineas reward is offered to any person that will make discovery and prosecute to conviction the thief or thieves that have stolen a grindstone from the King's wharf at Navy, between the 30th of April and the 6th instant. JOHN McGILL, *Com. of Stores, etc., for the Province of Upper Canada.* Queenstown, 16th May, 1793."
  Lieut.-Col. Simcoe always felt himself bound as much to protect the defenceless people in the country

as to make war on those in open rebellion.   An instance of this occurs in this campaign, on the occasion, in this month of March, when reports coming in of the enemy making a road through the Dismal Swamp, to the left of the great bridge, and small parties infesting the country, he sent Captain McKay out to disperse the enemy.   Captain McKay entered on the enterprise with spirit and resolution, altogether in a soldier-like manner.   Lieut.-Col. Simcoe, in public orders, thought proper to mark his appreciation of the conduct of the force in the following terms :—" It is with great pleasure the Lieutenant-Colonel hears of the orderly and soldier-like behaviour of the whole party stationed at Kemps.   He hopes the regiment will equally pride themselves in protecting, as in the present case, un-armed inhabitants of the country, as in scourging the armed banditti who oppress it."

On the 19th March, on information of a squadron with French colours being at anchor in Lynnhaven Bay, Lieut.-Col. Simcoe was sent there with a parole to observe them.   He had the pleasure to find that it was Admiral Arbuthnot's fleet, and of seeing a rebel cruiser, deceived by their colours, taken by them.   The action which the Admiral had with the French fleet saved the armament in Virginia from a serious attack.

Early in April, 1781, the Americans being in pos-session of Yorktown, means were taken to dislodge them. General Phillips had command of the force charged with the carrying out of this project, but Lieut.-Col. Simcoe and the Rangers took part in this affair, Lieut.-Col. Simcoe being the first to enter the town, when he directed the guns of the batteries that the Americans had already loaded to be fired, as a signal to the *Bonetta* sloop, which sailed up and anchored off the town, and he burnt a range of the rebel barracks. It is one thing to take a town and another thing to hold it, as we shall see in the sequel.

The next expedition we have to notice is that made for the purpose of taking Petersburgh and destroying the public stores at that place. Major-General Phillips issued orders directing the movement the expedition was to make. *Inter alia* he said, "The march will be conducted with the greatest caution, and the soldiers will pay the strictest obedience to orders; the conduct of the officers is not to be doubted. When the troops form, it is to be done in the following manner: The Infantry and Hussars of the Queen's Rangers, with a detachment of Yagers and Althause's Rifle Company, form the advanced guard, under Lieut.-Col. Simcoe. . . . The Cavalry of the Queen's Rangers to form with the reserve, till such time as they may be called upon, on the wing of the first or second line."

The result of the expedition was that Petersburgh fell on the 20th April. The enemy were said to have lost near a hundred men, killed and wounded, while that of the British was only one man killed and ten wounded of the light infantry. On the 25th May we find the whole army, the Queen's Rangers included, at Petersburgh, under the command of General Earl Cornwallis.·

.   Up to this time in this campaign, until the final disaster of York Town, the British troops had been generally successful in their encounters with the enemy. The Queen's Rangers had done great service, as was admitted by everyone, friend and foe alike. After the 20th May and up to the 26th of June, the regiment was constantly on the alert, moving here, there and everywhere in the coast district of Virginia ; capturing men, out-posts, stores, and munitions of war of the enemy. It was a succession of pursuits, ambuscades, night attack and day attack, culminating in the action at Spencer's Ordinary, on the 26th June, and in a complete victory. There were many valiant deeds in this action. I will quote from Lieut.-Col. Simcoe's journal in regard to it, not only on account of its intrinsic value, but because several names are mentioned familiar to Canadian ears, names of men who themselves or whose kin had afterwards a name also in Upper Canada when Lieut.-Col. Simcoe became Lieut.-Governor. The Journal says :—" The Grenadier Company commanded by *Captain McGill*, signalized by their gallantry as well as by their dress, lost several valuable men. Captain Stevenson was distinguished as usual ; his chosen and well-trained infantry were obstinately opposed, but they carried their point with a loss of a fourth of their men killed and wounded. An' affair of this nature necessarily afforded a great variety of gallant actions in individuals. Captain McRae reported to Lieut.-Col. Simcoe that his subaltern, Lieut. Charles Dunlop, who had served in the Queen's Rangers from thirteen years of age, led on his division on horseback without suffering a man to fire, watching the enemy and giving a signal to his men to lay down whenever a party of them was about to fire.. : . . The whole of the loss of the Queen's Rangers amounted to ten killed and twenty-three wounded ; among the latter were Lieut. Swift Armstrong and Ensign Jarvis, acting with the Grenadiers. The Yagers had two or three men wounded and one killed. It may be supposed, in the course of so long a service, there was scarcely a man of them whose death did not call forth a variety of situations, in which his courage had been distinguished or his value exemplified, and it seemed to every one as if the flower of the regiment had been cut off. As the whole series of the service of light troops gives the greatest latitude for the exertion of individual talents and of individual courage, so did the present situation require the most perfect combination of them. Every division, every officer, every soldier, had his share in the merit of the action ; mistake in one might have brought on cowardice in the other, and a single panic-stricken soldier would probably have infected a platoon, and led to the utmost confusion and ruin; so that Lieut.-Col. Simcoe has ever considered this action as the climax of a campaign of five years ; as the result of true discipline, acquired in that space by unremitted diligence, toil and danger; as an honourable victory earned by veteran intrepidity."

Respecting this engagement Lord Cornwallis, on the 28th June, gave out in public orders, that " Lord Cornwallis desires Lieut.-Col. Simcoe will accept of his warmest acknowledgments for his spirited and judicious conduct in the action of the 26th instant, when he repulsed and defeated so superior a force of the enemy. He desires that Lieut.-Col. Simcoe will communicate his thanks to the officers and soldiers of the Queen's Rangers, and to Captain Ewald and the detachment of Yagers."

On this same day, 28th June, Lieut.-Col. Simcoe with the cavalry escorted Lord Cornwallis to Yorktown. The enemy fired a random shot or two from Gloucester at the escort when it marched into Yorktown, and were prepared to repeat it on its return, but this was avoided by keeping to the heights. The Queen's Rangers were employed principally at about this time in feeling for the main body of the enemy. Lieut.-Col. Simcoe often went out with a party, and, after proceeding several miles, allowing the larger part of his accompanying force to return, he himself, with a small escort, cautiously continued the march, with his cavalry only, through by-paths and woods in order the better to conceal his operations, and carefully felt the enemy's position to discover the disposition of his force.

On the 20th July the Rangers were at Portsmouth. There they embarked in vessels, and it was supposed they were intended to co-operate in an attack on Philadelphia. It was countermanded, and the troops sailing up the river, landed at Yorktown on the 2nd August. Several patrols were made from Yorktown to Williamsburg, by the cavalry of the Queen's Rangers under the command of Captain Shank, the health of Lieut.-Col. Simcoe being much impaired. This Captain Shank was the same Captain Shank who afterwards, during Lieut.-Col. Simcoe's reign as Governor of Upper Canada, settled at York (Toronto), and acquired there a large tract of land in what is now the western part of that city, in the vicinity of Bathurst Street.

Before proceeding further in the relation of the events of this period, I think it right to go back a little —which is excusable if for no other purpose than to make reference to another Canadian who distinguished himself in the Revolutionary War. I have before mentioned Captain Saunders' Cavalry Corps. This corps did good service in many ways, especially in Leslie's expedition in the spring of this year. Captain Saunders, at the close of the expedition, communicated with Lieut.-Col. Simcoe by letter, detailing the movements and incidents which had taken place while he was absent on that service. In this communication he specially mentions Cornet Merritt, of the corps, who had been a member of it when Lieut. Wilson was in command of this body of cavalry, before he himself was appointed to the command. Cornet Merritt, in the beginning of March, had been sent with a flag to carry a letter to General Marion, and was detained as a prisoner in retaliation for the detention of one Captain Postell. The communication proceeds :—

" They crammed Merritt, with about twenty others, sergeants and privates of different British regiments, in a small, nasty, dark place, made of logs, called a bull-pen ; but it was not long before he determined to extricate himself and his fellow-prisoners, which he thus effected : After having communicated his intention to them, and found them ready to support him, he pitched upon the strongest and most daring soldier, and having waited some days for a favourable opportunity, he observed that his guards (militia) were much alarmed, which he found was occasioned by a party of British having come into the neighbourhood. He then ordered this soldier to seize the sentry, who was posted at a small square hole cut through the logs, and which singly served the double purpose of door and window, which he instantly executed, drawing the astonished sentry to the hole with one hand, and threatening to cut his throat with a large knife which he held in the other, if he made the smallest resistance or outcry. Then Cornet Merritt and the whole party crawled out, the one after the other, undiscovered by the guard, though it was in the daytime, until the whole had got out. He then drew them up, which the officer of the guard observing, got his men under arms as fast as he could, and threatened to fire on them if they attempted to go off. Merritt replied that, if he dared to fire a single shot at him, he would cut the whole of his guard to pieces, which so intimidated him that, although Merritt's party was armed only with the spoils of the sentry and with clubs, yet he permitted them to march off unmolested to a river at some distance, where Cornet Merritt knew, from conversation which he had had with the sentries, that there was a large rice-boat, in which he embarked and brought his party, through a country of about fifty miles, safe into Georgetown. To you the undaunted bravery and spirit of this young man is not unknown; they obtained for him in his distress your friendship and protection."

Col. Balfour, in a letter approving of Merritt's

conduct on this occasion, said, " I rejoice most sincerely that your Cornet has escaped. His conduct and resolution do him great credit."

Col. Balfour again, when Captain Saunders was in command of this corps of cavalry at Georgetown, in the month of April, wrote to him and said, " Being empowered by Lord Cornwallis to raise a troop of Provincial light dragoons, I have for some time wished to try your Lieut. Wilson as Captain, and this gentleman (Merritt) as Lieutenant. They have both been recommended as good and active officers, and if you agree with me that a troop could be raised in or near Georgetown, I should have no hesitation in making the appointments."

Cornet Merritt was Cornet Thomas Merritt, the father of the well-known patriot, the late William Hamilton Merritt, of St. Catharines, a former member of the Parliament of Upper Canada, and projector of that great work, the Welland Canal. William Hamilton Merritt seems to have inherited his father's love for the cavalry, performing distinguished service as commander of the militia cavalry of Upper Canada in the War of 1812.

On the 31st August, 1781, the advance ships of the French fleet blockaded the river York. General Washington, on the 23rd September, invested Yorktown, occupied by the British under the command of

Lord Cornwallis. Lieut.-Col. Simcoe, still in command of the Rangers, was in bad health. His robust strength was shattered by the incessant fatigues, both of body and mind, which for years he had undergone. While lying on a sick bed he was informed that Lieut.-Col. Tarleton had marched out with the cavalry. About mid-day firing was heard in the direction taken by the cavalry. Some people galloped in in great confusion, one of the forage masters saying Col. Tarleton was defeated. Lieut.-Col. Simcoe sent him to Lord Cornwallis, ordered the troops to the front, and being carried from his bed to his horse, went himself to the redoubt occupied by the Rangers.

The fortunes of war were now against the British. The enemy were in greatly superior numbers. The works at Yorktown were rendered untenable by the superior fire of the French. Lord Cornwallis determined to evacuate the place and draw off his troops by way of Gloucester, and a principal part of his force was sent over to that place. A violent storm arising, prevented the succeeding division of the garrison of Yorktown passing over; the first division which had arrived returned to Yorktown, and the firing soon after ceasing, the news came that Cornwallis had proposed a cessation of hostilities, for the purpose of settling the terms on which the posts of York and Gloucester were to be surrendered. The capitulation was signed

on the 19th October.   On account of Lieut.-Col.
Simcoe's dangerous state of health, Cornwallis permitted him to sail for New York in the *Bonetta*,
which by an article in the capitulation was to be
left at his disposal, a sea-voyage being the only
chance, in the opinion of the physicians, by which he
could save his life.   On board of this vessel sailed as
many of the Rangers, and other corps, deserters from
the enemy, as she could possibly hold.   They were to
be exchanged as prisoners of war, and the remainder
of Cornwallis' army were marched prisoners into the
country.   Lieut.-Col. Simcoe, on his arrival in New
York, was permitted by Sir Henry Clinton to return to
England ; and His Majesty was graciously pleased, on
the 19th December, 1781, to confer upon him the rank
of Lieutenant-Colonel in the army, the duties and title
of which he had enjoyed from the year 1777, and which
had been made permanent to him in America in 1779.

Soon after the preliminaries of peace had been
signed, or at least divulged, in America, Lieut.-Col.
Simcoe received a testimonial which gave him great
pleasure and satisfaction.   The Associated Loyalists,
in the upper part of the Chesapeake, through an agent
and one of the principal of their number, presented
him with a written statement of the esteem in which
they held him.   The writer, on behalf of the Loyalists,
made his statement as follows :—

"I have the honour, on behalf of the deputies of the Associated Loyalists in Pennsylvania, Maryland, and the lower counties on the Delaware, by their particular direction, and being fully authorized by them for that purpose, now to express to you the high sense they entertain of your military and political conduct during the late rebellion in America. They are at a loss whether most to admire your activity and gallantry in the field or your generous and affectionate attachment to His Majesty's loyal subjects in America, and your unwearied exertions as well to promote their true interest as to preserve and protect their property.

"As they have with pleasure and satisfaction had frequent opportunities of seeing your army crowned with success, so have they as often experienced the marks of your favour, attention and protection ; these acts have endeared you to them and claim their warmest gratitude. Your particular countenance to and zeal for the Associated Loyalists, and your ready concurrence in the measures proposed for their relief, and kind solicitations on their behalf, have made an impression on their minds words cannot express and time only can erase ; and they have exceedingly to regret that the opportunity was not afforded them of evincing to the world, under your command, the sincerity of these professions and their attachment to their Sovereign.

"‚They would deem themselves culpable if they did not take this opportunity to mention that your abhorrence of the pillage that too generally took place in this country, and the success that attended your vigilant exertions to prevent it, have marked your character and ensured to you the esteem of all orders and ranks of good men.

" Your sudden and unexpected departure from America prevented their paying this tribute of respect to you personally, which they entreat you now to accept, and that you will be assured under all changes and circumstances your name will be dear to them, and that their wishes and prayers will always be for your prosperity and happiness."

The Queen's Rangers, under Lieut.-Col. Simcoe, it has already been shown, performed most distinguished service during the campaigns about which I have been writing. We have seen that His Majesty recognized the services of the Lieutenant-Colonel by making him Lieutenant-Colonel in the regular army ; nor did His Majesty forget the other officers of that regiment, for we find that on the 19th December, 1782, His Majesty was graciously pleased to make the rank of every officer of that regiment universally permanent, which they had hitherto only held in America, and the Queen's Rangers, cavalry and infantry, were honourably enrolled in the British army. The corps was disbanded at the ensuing peace, and many of the officers and most of the soldiers settled on the lands to which they had a claim in Nova Scotia. Many others of the force settled in Upper Canada, following the fortunes of their trusty leader.

Simcoe went to England on parole. Arriving there in bad health he left his case in the hands of ministers who, according to his Journal, did not neglect his interests in the matter of exchange and restoration to complete liberty. In the Appendix to his Journal, speaking of himself as he did invariably in the Journal in the third person, he says, " Lieut.-Col. Simcoe has always thought himself under the highest obligations to His Majesty's ministers for this mark of attention" (his exchange). The terms on which he was exchanged are here inserted, verbatim from Dr. Franklin's discharge : " Being informed by William Hodgson, Esquire, chairman of the committee of subscribers for the relief of American prisoners in England, of the benevolent and humane treatment lately received by the said prisoners in consequence of orders from the present British ministers ; and that the said ministers earnestly desire that Lieut.-Col. Simcoe, on parole to the United States of America, should be released from his said parole ; and being further of opinion that meeting the British Government in acts of benevolence is agreeable to the disposition and intention of the Congress, I do hereby,

as far as in my power may lie, absolve the parole of the
said Lieut.-Col. Simcoe, but on this condition,—that an
order be obtained for the discharge of some officer of
equal rank, who being a prisoner to the English in
America, shall be named by Congress or by General
Washington for that purpose, and that three copies of
such order be transmitted to me.

"Given at Passy, this 14th January 1783.

"B. FRANKLIN,

"*Minister Plenipotentiary from the United States of
America at the Court of France.*"

Thus was ended the military career of Lieut.-Col.
Simcoe—a man who during the whole of his military
life was honoured and beloved by all who knew him,
of most generous impulses and well entitled to promotion in the service of the Crown whose battles he
had fought, if with varying success, at least with
devotion and loyalty not surpassed by any of the
King's subjects of high or low degree.

CHAPTER VI.

CIVIL GOVERNMENT IN UPPER CANADA.

UPPER CANADA had its beginning as a separate province in 1791. The Act of the Imperial Parliament dividing the old Province of Quebec into the two Provinces of Upper and Lower Canada has generally been known as the 31st of the King. It was an Act of immense importance to the English-speaking people of the province, entailing far-reaching consequences to all who should make the new made Province of Upper Canada their future home. We have followed Lieut.-Col. Simcoe in his military career in the Revolution till it was brought to a close, and his return to England as a prisoner on parole, to his subsequent release, in 1783. Now in England, at his old home, enjoying a life of tranquillity, his mind was restored to its former tone, and his constitution to a state of health, which, if not perfect, was apparently so. Soon after retiring from active service he determined to change his condition in life, taking to himself for wife a Miss Guillem, a near relation of Admiral Graves who had commanded at Boston in the Revolution, and who was a distant relative of his own.

Lieut.-Col. Simcoe in 1790 was elected a member of the British Parliament to represent the borough of St. Maw's, Cornwall, and he took part in the debates on the Bill by which the Province of Quebec was divided into Upper and Lower Canada, the Constitutional Act of the 31st of the King to which I have referred. He had therefore an intimate knowledge of what was intended by that Bill, and of the course which the English Government desired to be pursued in the affairs of the then new and distinct Province of Upper Canada. No man better qualified to be Governor of this new Province than Simcoe could have been selected.

In the Revolutionary struggle he had associated himself with the Loyalists of America, and had become acquainted with their every want. He knew that when the struggle was over the Loyalists, unused and unwilling to live under the Republican Government, would flock into Canada, and thus escape the tyranny of the Sons of Liberty.

The better to understand this matter of the Act of 1791, and the circumstances attending it, I may state that the debate in the House of Commons on that Bill was commenced on the 8th April, 1791, and was championed by Mr. Pitt on the Government side of the House, and criticised by Mr. Fox, leader of the Opposition in the Commons. It is too important a matter to be in any way neglected in dealing with the the life of Lieut.-Col. Simcoe, the first Lieutenant-Governor appointed to administer government under it, so I state the facts as they appeared in the Journal of Parliament.

The order of the day being read for taking the report of the Quebec Government Bill into further consideration, Mr. Massey presented a petition from several merchants, warehousemen and manufacturers concerned in the trade of Quebec, praying that the Bill might not pass into a law, inasmuch as after having duly weighed the consequence of it, they conceived it would be attended with great injury to the said province, and particularly to the trade and commerce of the petitioners. It was ordered to lie on the table. The Speaker then put the question : " That this report be now taken into consideration."

Mr. Massey moved " That the Bill be recommitted." He made the motion because he thought there were many objections to various parts of the Bill.

Mr. Fox seconded the motion. He observed that the Bill contained a great variety of clauses, all of them of the utmost importance, not only to the country to which they immediately referred, but also to Great Britain. He hoped that in promulgating the scheme of a new constitution for the Province of Quebec the House would keep in their view those enlightened principles of freedom, which had always made a rapid progress over a considerable portion of the globe, and were becoming more and more every day universal. As the love of liberty was gaining ground in consequence of the diffusion of literature and knowledge through the world, he thought that a constitution should be formed for Canada as consistent as possible with the principles of freedom. This Bill, in his opinion, would not establish such a government, and that was his chief reason for opposing it.

The Bill proposed to give two Houses of Assembly in the two provinces, one to each of them, and thus far it met with his approbation, but the number of persons of whom these Assemblies were to consist deserved particular attention. Although it might be perfectly true, that a country, three or four times as large as Great Britain, ought to have representatives three or four times as numerous, yet it was not fit to say that a smaller country should have an Assembly proportionately small. The great object in the institution of all popular Assemblies was, that the people should be freely and fully represented, and that the representative body should have all the virtues and vices incidental to such Assemblies. But when they made an Assembly to consist of sixteen or thirty persons, they seemed to him to give a free Constitution in appearance, when in fact they withheld it. In Great Britain we had a Septennial Bill, but the goodness of it had been considered doubtful, at least, even by many of those who took a lead in the present Bill.

The Right Hon. the Chancellor of the Exchequer had himself supported a vote for the repeal of that Act. He did not now mean to discuss its merits ; but a main ground on which he thought it indispensable was that a general election in this country was attended with a variety of inconveniences. That general elections in Great Britain were attended with several inconveniences could not be doubted ; but when they came to a country so different in all circumstances as Canada, and where elections, for many years at least, were not likely to be attended with the consequences which they dreaded, why they should make such Assemblies not annual or triennial, but septennial, was beyond his comprehension. A Septennial Bill did not apply to many of the most respectable persons in that country ; they might be persons engaged in trade, and if chosen for seven years they might not be in a situation to attend during all that period ; their affairs might call them to England, or many other circumstances might arise effectually to prevent them from attending the service of their country. But although it might be inconvenient for such persons to attend such Assembly for the term of seven years, they might be able to give their attendance for one, or even for three years, without any danger or inconvenience to their commercial concerns. By a Septennial Bill the country of Canada might be deprived of many of the few representatives that were allowed by the Bill. If it should be said that this objection applied to Great Britain, he completely denied it ; because although there were persons engaged in trade in the British House of Commons, and many of them very worthy members, yet they were comparatively few ; and therefore he should think that, from the situation of Canada, annual or triennial parliaments would be much preferable to septennial.

Of the qualification of electors he felt it impossible to approve. In England a freeholder of forty-five shillings was sufficient ; five pounds was necessary in Canada. Perhaps it might be said that when this was fairly considered it would make no material difference ; and this he suspected to be the case. But granting that it did not, when we were giving to the world, by this Bill, our notions of the principles of elections, we should not hold out that the qualifications in Great Britain were lower than they ought to be. The qualifications on a house were still higher—he believed ten pounds.

In fact, he thought that the whole of this Constitution was an attempt to undermine and contradict the professed purport of the Bill, namely, the introduction of a popular Government into Canada.   But although this was the case with respect to the two Assemblies, although they were to consist of so inconsiderable a number of members, the legislative councils in both provinces were limited as to numbers.   Instead of being hereditary councils, or councils chosen by electors, as was the case in some of the colonies in the West Indies, or chosen by the King, they were compounded of the other two.   As to the points of hereditary honours, to say that they were good or that they were not good, as a general proposition, was not easily maintained ; but he saw nothing so good in hereditary powers and honours as to incline us to introduce them into a country where they were unknown, and by such means distinguish Canada from all the colonies in the West Indies.   In countries where they made a part of the Constitution, he did not think it wise to destroy, but to give birth and life to such principles in countries where they did not exist, appeared to him to be exceedingly unwise.   Nor could he account for it, unless it was that Canada having been formerly a French colony, there might be an opportunity of reviving those titles of honour the extinction of which some gentlemen so much deplored, and to revive in the west that spirit of chivalry which had fallen into disgrace in the neighbouring country. He asked if those red and blue ribbons, which had lost their lustre in the old world, were to shine forth again in the new ? It seemed to him peculiarly absurd to introduce hereditary honours in America, where those artificial distinctions stunk in the nostrils of the natives. He declared he thought these powers and honours wholly unnecessary, and tending to make a new Constitution worse rather than better. If the council were wholly hereditary he should equally object to it : it would only add to the power of the King and the Governor, for a council so formed would only be the tool and engine of the King. Here the Speaker, Mr. Fox, condemned the Clergy Reserves clauses of the Bill and the clause relating to appeals to the Privy Council instead of the House of Lords in the first instance, and then went on to say further, as to the Bill, that of all the points of the Bill, that which struck him the most forcibly was the division of the Province of Canada. It had been urged that, by such means, we could separate the English and French inhabitants of the province ; that we could distinguish who were originally French from those of English origin. But was this to be desired ? Was it not rather to be avoided ? Was it agreeable to general political expediency ? The most desirable circumstance was that the French and English inhabitants of Canada should coalesce as it were, in one body, and that the different distinctions of the people might be extinguished forever. If this had been the object in view, the English laws might have prevailed universally throughout Canada ; not from force, but from choice and conviction of their superiority. He had no doubt that, on a fair trial, they would be found free from all objection. The inhabitants of Canada had not the laws of France. The commercial code was never established there ; they stood upon the exceedingly inconvenient custom of Paris. He wished the people of that country to adopt the English laws from choice and not from force ; and he did not think the division of the province the most likely means to bring about this most desirable end. He trusted the House would also seriously consider the particular situation of Canada. It was not to be compared with the West Indies ; it was a country of a different nature ; it did not consist of a few white inhabitants and a number of slaves ; but it was a country of great growing population, which had increased very much, and which, he hoped, would increase much more. It was a country as capable of enjoying political freedom, in its utmost extent, as any other country on the face of the globe. This country was situated near the Colonies of North America. All their animosity and bitterness on the quarrel between them and Great Britain was now over, and he believed that there were few people among those colonies who would not be ready to admit every person belonging to this country into a participation of all their privileges, and would receive them with open arms. The governments now established in North America were, in his opinion, the best adapted to the situation of the people who lived under them of any of the governments of the ancient or modern world ; and when we had a colony like this, capable of freedom and capable of a great increase of population, it was material that the inhabitants should have nothing to look to among their neighbours to excite their envy. Canada must be preserved to Great Britain by the choice of its inhabitants.   But it should be felt by the inhabitants that their situation was not worse than that of their neighbours.   He wished the Canadians to be in such a situation as to have nothing to envy in any part of the King's dominions.   But this should never be the case under a Bill which held out to them something like the shadow of the British Constitution, but denied them the substance.   In a country where the principles of liberty were gaining ground, they should have a government as agreeable to the genuine principles of freedom as was consistent with the nature of the circumstances.   He did not think that the government intended to be established by this Bill would prove such a government ; and this was his principal

motive for opposing it.   The Legislative Council ought
to be totally free and repeatedly chosen, in a manner
as much independent of the Governor as the nature
of a colony would admit.   Those he conceived would
be the best, but, if not, they should have their seats
for life ; be appointed by the King ; consist of a
limited number, and possess no hereditary honours.
Those honours might be very proper, and of great
utility in countries where they had existed by long
custom, but, in his opinion, they were not fit to be
introduced where they had no original existence ; then
there was no particular use for introducing them,
arising from the nature of the country, its extent, its
state of improvement, or its peculiar circumstances,
where instead of attracting respect they might excite
envy ; and as but few could enjoy them, those who
did not, might be induced to form an unfavourable
comparison between their own situation and that of
their neighbours, among whom no such distinctions
were known.   It was upon these grounds which he had
stated that he felt himself justified in seconding the
motion of his honourable friend.

Mr. Pitt replied to Mr. Fox in a short address, in
which he endeavoured to strengthen the reasons he
pressed for the passing of the Bill when it was further
introduced, and added : " As to the Legislative Council,
he entirely differed from the Right Hon. gentleman,

who thought it would be better to be an elective council, in the manner in which it had been lately established in America.   An aristocratic principle being one part of our mixed Government, he thought proper that there should be such a council in Canada as was provided for by the Bill, and which might answer to that part of the British Constitution which composed the other House of Parliament.

"As to the division of the province, it was, in a great measure, the fundamental part of the Bill ; and he had no scruple to declare that he considered it as the most material and essential part of it."   He agreed with the Right Hon. gentleman in thinking it extremely desirable that the inhabitants of Canada should be united, and led universally to prefer the English Constitution and the English law.   Dividing the province he considered to be the most likely means to effect this purpose, since by so doing the French subjects would be sensible that the British Government had no intention of forcing the English laws upon them, and therefore they would with more facility look at the operation and effect of those laws, and probably in time adopt them from conviction.   This he thought was more likely to be the case than if the British Government were all at once to subject the whole inhabitants to the Constitution and laws of this country. Experience would teach them that the English laws were the best ; and he admitted that they ought to be governed to their satisfaction. If the province had not been divided there would have been only one House of Assembly ; and there being two parties, if those parties had been equal or nearly equal in the Assembly, it would have been the source of perpetual faction. If one of the parties had been much stronger than the other the other might justly have complained that they were oppressed. It was on that persuasion that the division of the province was conceived to be the most likely way of attaining every desirable end."

The Bill was then ordered to be recommitted. The Bill was debated clause by clause in committee on May 6th, 11th, 12th and 16th, and finally passed the second reading on the 16th May, 1791.

I am not able to state the exact date of the appointment of Lieut.-Col. Simcoe to the Lieutenant-Governorship of Upper Canada, but it must have been immediately on or immediately after the passing of the Act, for among the Smith manuscript papers, now deposited in the Public Library of Toronto, there is a letter, dated the 20th day of May, 1791, written by Lieut.-Col. Simcoe from some place in England (name of place not given) to D. W. Smith, afterwards Acting Surveyor-General of the province, in which he gives directions to him on matters which he deemed to be of public service, shewing also as it does an intelligent appreciation of the duties he was called upon to perform. The letter was as follows :—

" It being necessary for the public service that an analysis should be made of a salt spring, reported by the Surveyor-General to be on the river Trent, I have directed Mr. Angus Macdonell to proceed immediately to analyze its quality. He will receive particular instructions for this purpose . . . As soon as the expedition shall be over, be ready to report to me as soon as I shall arrive in Upper Canada."

The letter was indeed an order and very explicit in its directions. Particular care was taken to direct the surveyor to do nothing which would tend to make the Indians jealous or to lead them to think " that they will in any way be impeded from the customary resort to the salt springs. Furthermore directions were given that the surveyor should " note down as particularly as possible the nature of the soil and of the country he should pass through, or any other observations that may be serviceable to His Majesty's Government." The letter goes on to say : " If the experiment prove successful, it is much to be desired that a haven for small vessels be procured on Lake Ontario, opposite to the Presqu'Isle of Quinté."

In another letter of the same date he writes directing the party to whom it was addressed, but whose name is not given, " to proceed with Mr. Chewett to the salt springs on the river Trent, and to make a particular and methodical analysis of the salt spring and report to him (Lieut.-Col. Simcoe) at Kingston or wherever he should be."

These letters show that Lieut.-Col. Simcoe, from the moment he was appointed Governor of the province, even before setting foot on the soil, took a keen and lively interest in all that was likely to add to its welfare even in the smallest minutiæ. Referring to the salt spring there deemed of great importance, he says : "It being necessary for the *public service* that an analysis should be made of a salt spring." How could the newly-appointed Governor have known of a salt spring on the Trent unless he had made himself familiar with the written evidences in the hands of the Government, or by enquiry have satisfied himself that such spring existed? In those early days a salt spring was estimated of as much value, or nearly of as much value, as a gold mine.

Then again let it be noticed what paternal solicitude he evinces for the Indians : "Particular care is to be taken to do nothing which would tend to make the Indians jealous or to lead them to think that they will in any way be impeded from the customary resort to the salt spring." Not only was a salt spring prized for its intrinsic value, but because of the veneration in which it was held by the Indians. The Indians who lived by the hunt and the chase could not but deem of especial value these places where the animals they hunted for sport and sustenance came for their food and drink. Salt or lick springs were considered sacred by the Indiains because of their being the resort of the deer, the elk, the bear and the buffalo. It may have been that Governor Simcoe, in his experience gained in the Revolutionary War, knew of this almost superstitious regard which the Indians had for these springs, and therefore pressed upon his surveyors in the province the necessity of preserving them.

A delegation of warriors from the Delaware tribe having visited the Governor of Virginia during the Revolution on matters of business, the Governor asked them some questions relative to their country, and among others what they knew or had heard of the animal whose bones were found on the Salt Licks on the Ohio. Their chief speaker immediately put himself into an attitude of oratory, and with a pomp suited to what he conceived the elevation of his subject, informed him that it was a tradition, handed down from their fathers, that in ancient times a herd of these tremendous animals came to the Bick-Bone Licks, and began an universal destruction of the bear, deer, elk, buffalo, and other animals which had been created for the use of the Indians. " That the Great Man above, looking down and seeing this, he seized his lightning,

descended on the earth, seated himself on a neighbouring mountain, on a rock—on which his seat and
the prints of his feet are still to be seen,—and hurled
his bolts among them, until the whole were slaughtered
except the big bull, who, presenting his forehead to the
shafts, shook them off as they fell, but missing one, at
length, it wounded him in the side, whereupon, springing round, he bounded over the Ohio, over the Wabash,
the Illinois, and over the Great Lakes, where he is
living this day." The big bull here referred to is the
mammoth ; so that, according to the tradition, Canada
over the Great Lakes was made the home of this
tremendous animal.

Before Lieut.-Col. Simcoe left England his friend,
the Duke of Northumberland, himself a Chief, had no
doubt impressed him with the English policy of treating
the Indians, the original owners of the soil, with kindness and consideration. On the 3rd September, 1791,
the Duke gave him a letter to his brother Chief, Captain
Joseph Brant *(Thayendanegea)*, which I transcribe, as
indicative of the spirit which animated the breast of
the colonial minister voicing the sentiments of the
Crown as regarded the aborigines. The letter was as
follows :—

" NORTHUMBERLAND HOUSE,

" September 3rd, 1791.

" MY DEAR JOSEPH,——

"Col. Simcoe, who is going out as Governor of Upper Canada, is kind enough to promise to deliver this to you, with a brace of pistols which I desire you will keep for my sake. I must particularly recommend the Colonel to you and the nation. He is a most intimate friend of mine, and is possessed of every good quality which can recommend him to your friendship. He is brave, humane, sensible and honest. You may safely rely upon whatever he says, for he will not deceive you.

" He loves and honours the Indians, whose noble sentiments so perfectly correspond with his own. He wishes to live upon the best terms with them, and, as Governor, will have it in his power to be of much service to them. In. short, he is worthy to be a Mohawk. Love him at first for my sake and you will soon come to love him for his own.

" I was very glad to hear that you had received the rifle safe which I sent you, and hope it has proved useful to you. I preserve with great care your picture, which is hung up in the Duchess's own room.

" Continue to me your friendship and esteem, and believe me ever to be, with the greatest truth,

" Your affectionate friend and brother,

" NORTHUMBERLAND,

~

" *Thorighwegeri.*

" CAPTAIN JOSEPH BRANT,

" *Thayendenagea.*"

Governor Simcoe on setting out from England for his new government sailed for Quebec. We find him on the 17th January, 1792, at Montreal, *en route* for Kingston and Niagara. In a private letter of that date, addressed to Sir George Yonge, Secretary of War, in which he announced to him his arrival in Montreal, he reported that Captain Shaw had just successfully marched with his division of the Queen's Rangers all the way from New Brunswick to Montreal in the depth of winter on snow shoes. In this letter Captain David Shank is spoken of as being on his way to the same destination in command of a portion of the Queen's Rangers, in company with Captain Smith.

The Captain Shaw here referred to was Captain Æneas Shaw (who became a resident of York), the great-grand father of Col. Shaw, late of the 10th Royal Regiment, now called the Royal Grenadiers. The Captain Smith referred to was afterwards Col. Samuel

Smith, appointed a member of the Executive Council in 1815, and subsequently President of the Province. Captain David Shank and his position I have referred to in the military life of Governor Simcoe. I have mentioned that on leaving Montreal the Governor was *en route* for Kingston and Niagara. The ordinary way of travelling up the River St. Lawrence in those days was by bark canoe. Governor Simcoe, in ascending the river, had a fleet of bark canoes. On the way up the party stopped at a hostelry at Johnstown. From the fact that the Governor and his party stopped there on the occasion of his coming to the province as its Governor the hostelry obtained quite a local importance. It is described as St. John's Hall, and the usual sign is not on the building, but at the top of a tapering pine. The inscription on the sign was : " Live and let live—peace and plenty to all mankind." The name of the Hall (St. John's), would seem to indicate that there were a good many Masons in that part of the country. In this house Governor Simcoe held his first levee in Upper Canada. He was received by the inhabitants of the neighbouring country, who assembled there to attest their loyalty, with a salvo of artillery, the ordnance used for the occasion being an old cannon obtained from the old French Fort on the Island below Johnstown. Soon after the Governor left on his journey up the river, the gentry of the surrounding country, in their queer old broad-skirted military coats, their low tasseled boots, their looped chapeaux, with faded feathers fluttering in the wind, collected together, retired to St. John's Hall, and there did honour to the occasion in speech making and health drinking, as was the custom of the time. The names of those who attended that meeting are quite familiar to me, born, and living in my boyhood, not far from the homes of the gentry assembled, some of whom I knew personally. In the speech-making Col. Tom Fraser said, " Now I am content—content, I say, and can go home to reflect on this proud day. Our Governor, the man of all others, has come at last. Mine eyes have seen it—a health to him, gentlemen—he will do the best for us." Those who assisted the eloquent Colonel Fraser in chanting his *Nunc Dimittis* were : Dr. Solomon Jones, Captain Elijah Bottum, Major Jessop, Captain Dulmage, Captain Campbell, Paymaster Jones, Commissary Jones, Captain Gid Adams, Lieut. Samuel Adams, Ephraim Webster, Captain Markle, Captain Grant and numerous other officers.

After leaving Johnstown the fleet ascended the river, and in due time reached Kingston, the first fortified place met with in journeying from Montreal to Niagara. It was here that the Governor in 1791 first organized his government, by selecting his Executive and Legislative Council. The organization and the ceremonies on the occasion partook of a religious character. The event was one of solemnity ; the place, the old wooden church opposite the market place, Kingston. Here in this church were read and published His Majesty's commissions. The Governor was attended by the Honourable William Osgoode, C.J., the Honourable James Baby, the Honourable Peter Russell, together with the Justices of the Peace and principal inhabitants, when the commission appointing His Excellency Lord Dorchester, Captain-General and Commander-in-chief, etc., of Upper Canada and Lower Canada, and John Graves Simcoe, Governor of the Province of Upper Canada, was solemnly read and published. The oaths of office were then administered to His Excellency. According to the Royal instructions to General Simcoe he was to have five individuals to form his first Executive Council. The five named were : William Osgoode, William Robertson, James Baby, Alexander Grant and Peter Russell, Esquires. These appointments were made on the 8th July. On the following Monday, Messrs. Osgoode, Russell and Baby were sworn into office ; Robertson was not then in the province ; Grant was sworn in a few days afterwards.

The Legislative Councillors were not selected till 17th July, 1792, when a meeting of the Executive Council was held at Kingston, and the following gentlemen appointed : Robert Hamilton, Richard Cartwright and John Munro.

Kingston, at the foot of Lake Ontario, which in the old French days had an historic name, being a military post, the Governor, being a military man, appropriately seized upon as a fit place where he might announce to the inhabitants of the province that the first Governor of the province was in their midst.

Fort Frontenac, the Kingston of the time of the arrival of Governor Simcoe and of the present day, was captured by the English under Colonel Bradstreet, in 1758, a year before the fall of Quebec. The history of the time points to the fact that Governor Simcoe sojourned during the winter in Montreal, and did no leave that place till May or June, 1792. I have seen a sketch, a water-colour drawing of Sorel, made by Mrs. Simcoe, on the back of which is written, " Sorel, 12th June, 1792," which shows that the Governor was either in Montreal or Sorel at that date.

In a letter written by Governor Simcoe to the Secretary of War, on the 13th June, 1792, he mentioned that "Captain Littlehales has overtaken me on the St. Lawrence as I was on my passage up the most august of rivers (St. Lawrence). It has given me great satisfaction," he says, " that the Queen's Rangers have arrived so early. Captain Shaw, who crossed in the depth of winter on showshoes from New Brunswick, is now at Kingston with the troops of the first two ships ; and Captains Shank and Smith are, I trust, at no great distance from this place, as the wind has served for the last thirty-six hours, and I hope with sufficient force to enable them to pass the rapids of the Richelieu, where they have been detained some days."

These letters show that the Governor was slowly but surely making his way to Niagara, where there was another fort, and that he had not come to the province without military support, for we see that the "Queen's Rangers," his old regiment reorganized, were on the way with him, and in command of officers who had been with him in the Revolutionary War. Captains Shaw and Smith had with him gone through all the campaigns of the Revolutionary War.

Mrs. Simcoe, who accompanied the Governor on his journey, was something of an artist. She could draw and paint well, was a good maker of maps, and was an accomplished and accurate artist. She was not idle in making her journey up the St. Lawrence, but occupied herself in making pencil and water-colour drawings of the principal places, mountains and plains she passed on her way up the rapids of the St. Lawrence, not omitting the rapids themselves. That the reader may have an idea of some of these places and scenes, as sketched by Mrs. Simcoe, I give in the illustrations some woodcuts of Mrs. Simcoe's original sketches, which I have been enabled to secure through the kindness of Mr. Isidore Hellmuth, of London.

The Government being now organized (July, 1792), we may close this chapter and proceed in the next to say something of the country and people the Governor came to govern, first remarking that the Governor left Kingston, for his new capital of Newark, on 21st July, 1792.

CHAPTER VII.

THE FIRST PARLIAMENT OF UPPER CANADA.

THE Governor is now, 1792, at Newark (Niagara), his seat of Government for the present, at least. How Newark became the Capital it is hardly necessary to enquire. It is sufficient to know that the Governor on coming to the Province made this place his headquarters, and summoned his first parliament to meet him at Newark. The place itself was but a village of some four hundred houses, but then opposite on the point was old Fort Niagara, which had alternately belonged to the French, and to the English, and was now in possession of the English, as one of the trading posts retained by the English notwithstanding the treaty of 1783, which granted to the United States their independence. The British, in consequence of a claim made by them that the Americans had not carried out some stipulation of the treaty, held the trading posts of Niagara and Detroit till another treaty, called the Jay Treaty, was made in 1796.

Newark was well protected by the guns of Fort Niagara; that and other considerations, such as the

PORTRAIT OF WILLIAM JARVIS.

From an original Painting by Sir Thomas Lawrence.

fact that many of the Loyalists of the Queen's and Butler's Rangers, after the treaty of 1783, came to Upper Canada, and pitched their tents on the Niagara peninsula induced the Governor to make Newark his capital. Governor Simcoe would thus at Newark find himself, as it were, among his own people. But the settlers on the Niagara peninsula were not the only people of Upper Canada at this time. In addition, there were about ten thousand English-speaking people, and about ten thousand Indians in the province. The body of the people were, however, settled over widely scattered districts. The U. E. Loyalists, who came into the province after losing their all in the revolted colonies, were glad to procure a resting place wherever fortune or accident landed them. Some parties entered the province at this place, some another. A number came in by crossing the St. Lawrence in the vicinity of Cornwall ; others at Montreal ; others again, would land at Cataraqui or Kingston ; the greater number perhaps on the Niagara frontier.

When one is writing the history of a governor it is as well to know who were the people he came to govern, if a just conclusion as to the Governor's merit is to be arrived at.

Governor Simcoe was fortunate in coming among a people who had all the refinements of the civilization of the old colonies from which they had been driven by the chances of war. Many had left their American firesides and hearthstones because of their devoted loyalty to the King and monarchical government. They had been inured to the hardships of the war, and were therefore prepared to be watchful and patient. They were not novices in the art of agriculture, the most of them leaving good, well-cultivated farms on coming to Canada. Nor were they without the refinements of education; having had the advantage of the schools of New England and other States, which were as good and efficient at that time as were the schools of Canada at the expiry of fifty years of their settlement in Upper Canada.

The United Empire Loyalists were the principal inhabitants of the Province. Still there were others besides the Indians that the Governor had within his jurisdiction. There were the settlers around the posts and fortified places, discharged soldiers, and others who, for security from the Indians, chose to settle on land in the vicinity of these places. As far back as the time of the attacks on the British posts by the great Chief Pontiac there is evidence that persons were placed in charge of these out-posts and forts about Frontenac. These men invariably received grants of land and thus formed the sparse beginnings of settlements. The province had since its settlement in 1784 been under the jurisdiction of Governor Haldimand and the Legislature of Lower Canada, which was founded by the Quebec Act of 1774. In 1784 Governor Haldimand had settled the celebrated Iroquois Chief, Thayend-anegea, Joseph Brant, with his Indians, who had followed the fortunes of Britain, on a reserve granted to them on the banks of the Grand River. This grant of Governor Haldimand was dated 25th October, 1784, and was made to the Mohawk tribe. Another reserve was assigned the Mohawk tribe of Indians on the Grand River by Governor Simcoe on the 14th January, 1793. Both of these grants are on record in the office of the Provincial Secretary.

As to the country itself, it was essentially a woodland country ; a country of native forest trees and uncultivated land, in fact, almost a wilderness, when Governor Simcoe first entered it as Governor. There were settlements here and there which the U. E. Loyalists had formed in distant parts of the province, where they had felled the large trees and in some manner subjugated the soil—but they were few and far between. So late as 1812 the venerable William Ryerson, when aide-de-camp to a British General during the war of 1812, was sent on a message from the River St. Clair to Little York, now Toronto, and his road through all that country was but an Indian track through unbroken forests. When we come to tell of Governor Simcoe being fully installed as Governor, and his first session of 'Parliament, we may be able to describe his journey through the same territory, and see how he found it.

Coming to a country in such a primitive, almost primæval, state as Upper Canada was at this time it will be confessed the Governor had no ordinary task to perform, to produce form out of chaos, and put the machinery of government in good working order. It required a man of good mind, sober judgment, and great discretion to adapt himself to the state of affairs he found in Upper Canada.

The Governor, on assuming the duties of government, was especially interested in having around him a set of officials in whom he himself personally could have the utmost confidence, and whom he felt would loyally support him in carrying out the instructions he had received from his master, the King. In those days of colonial government the Governor was King, so far as the colony was concerned. The principles of colonial government as they exist at the present day were not understood at that time, or if understood, were not practised. There was, in fact, no responsible government as there is now. The Governor himself did not acknowledge any responsibility but to the government that appointed him, while his officials assisting him to carry on the government were his nominees, acknowledging no responsibility to the people's representatives, but only to the Governor and the Crown. Thus it was that a great responsibility was thrown upon the Governor in the choice of his officers. Let us now see how he exercised his office in this particular. He chose for his Military. Secretary Major Littlehales, an officer of acknowledged merit and ability, who afterwards was for some time Secretary of War for Ireland during the Lord-Lieutenancy of the Marquis of Cornwallis. One of his Aides-de-Camps was Thomas Talbot, the Col. Talbot so well and long known in the province as the founder of the Talbot settlement in the western district, and who had been an officer in the Queen's Rangers. Mr. Gray was appointed Solicitor-General.

The Clerk of the Executive Council was Mr. Small, the head of the family of Small in York and Toronto. For Civil Secretary he had William Jarvis, generally known as Mr. Secretary Jarvis, who had also been an officer in the Rangers. Peter Russell was appointed Receiver-General ; D. W. Smith Surveyor-General ; and Thomas Ridout and William Chewett, Assistant Receivers-General. Thomas Ridout was the father of Thomas G. Ridout, formerly Cashier of the Bank of Upper Canada, and long known in the province as a distinguished citizen and Masonic Grand Master. William Jarvis was the first Grand Master of the Masonic order in the province. D. W. Smith was in 1779 an Ensign in the 5th Regiment of Foot.   He was in 1790 secretary of the Land Board of Detroit, and held many other offices, civil and military, at that place.   In the same year of 1792 that he was appointed Surveyor-General, he was also appointed Deputy Quartermaster-General and Secretary to Commodore Dante.   He was Deputy Judge Advocate and member of all the Land Boards and Vice-President of the Agricultural Society.   In 1793 he was articled to the Attorney-General and was called to the Bar in 1794.   He was a Privy Councillor in 1796, Deputy Lieutenant for the County of Lincoln, and Member of the Second Parliament; and from that time down to the 28th September, 1836, he held a great many civil and political offices in the Dominion.   This is the D. W. Smith whose manuscripts have been secured for the Public Library in Toronto.

From the names I have given it will be seen that the Governor selected for his subordinates gentlemen of acknowledged respectability and worth, many of whom had like himself been active in support of the King in the Revolutionary War.

Let us now see who were returned to the First Parliament of the province, which was opened at Newark on the 17th September, 1792.   Referring to the Constitutional Act of 1791, we find that that Act entitled the province to send fifteen members to the

Legislative Assembly. The names of the fifteen returned as representatives of the people in the first Assembly were: John Macdonell, who was elected Speaker; John Booth; Mr. Baby; Alexander Campbell; Philip Dorland, who, being a Quaker, would not be sworn in, and did not take his seat; Peter Vanalstine, elected in Mr. Dorland's place; Jeremiah French; Ephraim Jones; William Macomb; Hugh Macdonell; Benjamin Rawling; Nathaniel Pettit; David William Smith; Hazelton Spencer; Isaac Swayzy; — Young; John White.

John White was the first Attorney-General of the province. In his day duelling was the fashionable way of settling personal affront. Following the custom the Attorney-General, on January 3rd, 1800, fought a duel with Mr. John Small, the Clerk of the Executive Council, and received a wound from which he died a few days afterwards.

The Governor had called the House together for the 17th September, little thinking at the time the call was made that circumstances might arise which would prevent many of the members attending. This, however, turned out to be the case. The settlers of these days could not afford just at this season, when they were housing their crops and doing their fall work, to leave their homes, although it might be to perform Parliamentary duties.

Looking back to these times, we cannot altogether realize, but are able to conjecture, the pride gentlemen of the Commons must have felt in being summoned to legislate on provincial affairs. Those were Arcadian days, when the demon of Party had not yet appeared to disturb the tranquillity of a united people. It was with difficulty that members reached Newark in time to answer the roll-call. Still they gathered in sufficient numbers to enable His Excellency to open the House on the day named. Governor Simcoe was present, as we may suppose in military uniform, soldier as he was, to receive his faithful Commons come to hear the first speech of the Governor of the newly constituted province.

· The Governor, in order to impress the province with the fact that it had become an offshoot of the great Empire whose servant he was, determined to open Parliament with all the ceremonial that distinguished the opening of the English Parliament, as far as the same could be adapted to the condition of the colony.

Niagara was still, as one of the posts retained by the British, as previously mentioned, garrisoned by British troops. Then the Governor had with him the Queen's Rangers, which had followed him from England. This was not the old corps of Queen's Rangers that he had commanded during the Revolutionary War, but a new regiment with the old name, raised for colonial service, many of the officers of which were companions-in-arms with Governor Simcoe during the Revolutionary struggle.

At the opening of the House soldiers were drawn from the fort to act as guard of honour to His Excellency, and to accompany him to the place of meeting of the Assembly. It was something novel for the few people and Indians then gathered to witness the pageant of a military Governor, attended by his Staff, proceeding to perform the solemn act of dedicating, as it were, an outlying province to the care of representatives called together to deliberate on affairs concerning the weal or woe of the future inhabitants of the province.

In opening the House, His Excellency delivered the following speech :—

"*Honourable Gentlemen of the Legislative Council and Gentlemen of the House of Assembly :*

"I have summoned you together under the authority of an Act of Parliament of Great Britain, passed in the last year, which has established the British Constitution and all the forms which secure and maintain it in this distant country.

"The wisdom and beneficence of our Most Gracious Sovereign and the British Parliament have been eminently proved, not only in imparting to us the same form of government, but in securing the benefit by the many provisions which guard this memorable Act, so that the blessings of our invulnerable Constitution, thus protected and amplified, we hope will be extended to the remotest posterity.

"The great and momentous trusts and duties which have been committed to the representatives of this province, in a degree infinitely beyond whatever till this period have distinguished any other colony, have originated from the British nation upon a just consideration of the energy and hazard with which the inhabitants have so conspicuously supported and defended the British Constitution.

"It is from the same patriotism now called upon to exercise, with due deliberation and foresight, the various offices of the civil administration that your fellow-subjects of the British Empire expect the foundation of union, of industry and wealth, of commerce and power, which may last through all succeeding ages. The natural advantages of the Province of Upper Canada are inferior to none on this side of the Atlantic. There can be no separate interest through its whole extent. The British form of government has prepared the way for its speedy colonization, and I trust that your fostering care will improve the favourable situation, and that a numerous and agricultural people will speedily take possession of a soil and climate, which, under the British laws and the munificence with which

His Majesty has granted the lands of the Crown, offer such manifest and peculiar encouragements."

It will be seen from this address that the Governor treated Upper Canada as the most favoured of colonies. He speaks of " the great and momentous trusts and duties which have been committed to the representatives of this province, in a degree infinitely beyond what, till this period, have distinguished any other colony." . Then he refers to "the energy and hazard with which they had so conspicuously supported and defended the British constitution "— evidently alluding to the sacrifices made by the United Empire Loyalists during the American Revolution.

The British Constitution was, in the mind of the Governor, superior to all other constitutions. He referred to it more than once during his address, and in terms which must have fired the members with new hopes and aspirations for their future home. Up to this time they had been under French rule and French or French-Canadian laws, as imposed by the Quebec Act of 1774 ; but now they were released from their thraldom and were to be under a government modelled after the form of the old British Constitution, and that government was to be administered by a Governor, who, above most other men, placed a high value upon the privileges and liberty guaranteed by that Constitution.

The legislators, profiting by the Governor's expression of admiration for the Constitution, at once set about legislating, and passed "An Act to repeal certain parts of an Act passed in the fourteenth year of His Majesty's reign, entitled, 'An Act for making more effectual provision for the government of the Province of Quebec, in North America,' and to introduce the English law as the Rule of Decision in all matters of controversy, relative to property and civil rights." This Act may be said to be the great charter of the people's liberty in Upper Canada, as it was under it that the law of England was made to supersede the old laws of Canada founded on the French civil law.

Following up the determination of the Legislature to be governed by English law, and by that only, the next Act passed by this First Parliament was, "An Act to establish Trial by Jury."

There were only eight Acts passed this session, but they were Acts of a practical character, and such as were required for the early development of a new province, working under a new constitution. The first session of the Legislature lasted till the 15th of October, 1792, or for a period less than a month by two days, when it was prorogued by His Excellency after he had, in the accustomed form, thanked the members for the legislation they had perfected.

A RELIC OF OLD NAVY HALL (Newark), NIAGARA

From a water-colour drawing by Miss Roberts, 1889.

CHAPTER VIII.

VISIT TO DETROIT AND THE MOHAWKS.

NO sooner had the Legislature been prorogued than the Governor set about giving directions to his officers on matters relative to the development of the province. There is among the Smith manuscripts an autograph letter of the Governor, written from Navy Hall to D. W. Smith, Acting Surveyor-General, Upper Canada, drawing his attention to the care which should be observed in guarding the interests of the Crown in regard to mill sites.

"Navy Hall," at the top of this letter, reminds us that Navy Hall was the name of the residence of the Governor in Newark. It was a plain frame building, and until taken possession of by the Governor, on his arrival in Newark, had been used for the housing of navy stores—that is, stores of the Government for use in the lake navy, which consisted of vessels of war adapted to the navigation of Lake Ontario, and manned by men from the Royal Navy.

.   Speculation has been indulged in as to where
Navy Hall really was located.   I have procured from
the archives at Ottawa information which establishes
without doubt that the site of the Hall was on the
bank of the Niagara River, just under where Fort
George stands.   The Fort, which is a wreck of what it
was, was constructed nearly a century ago, and was one
of the forts in the system of fortifications intended to
counteract the designs of an enemy on the old Fort
Niagara on the opposite side of the river.

In a report by Gother Mann, commanding the
Royal Engineers, dated the 22nd September, 1789, on
the state of the fortifications, etc., Niagara and Navy
Hall are reported upon together.   After referring to
Fort Niagara and the re-establishing of the north demi-
bastion, which had been greatly damaged and partly
washed away by the fury of the lake, the report goes on
to state: "A survey of the heights also, on the opposite
side of the river about Navy Hall, has been made
with a view to ascertain the best system for fortifying
the same so as to establish a permanent post there, and
which might also counteract the designs of an enemy
in his attack on the Fort of Niagara."

Again, on the 1st March, 1790, Mann reports
"that the space on which Fort Niagara stands is
diminishing from the depredations of the lake"; and
as to Navy Hall, "that the ground above Navy Hall,

if chosen for a principal post, will admit a wall of good capacity, but, as it will be retired from the river, there must be subordinate batteries on the banks thereof to command the passage ; it will be about sixteen hundred yards distant from the Fort at Niagara, which, though within the distance of annoying an enemy, could not prevent his carrying on operations against the Fort."

It was on the report of Gother Mann that the ground above Navy Hall, was chosen as the site of Fort George. Navy Hall itself was not so much a building as a cluster or group of buildings. The map of Newark, in the Smith collection of papers, Public Library, Toronto, proves this to have been the case. This map, prepared by Mr. Chewett in 1804, shows four buildings as comprising Navy Hall. One of these buildings was a long structure, standing at right-angles to the river, and there were three others just beside this main building to the north-west, and built parallel with the river.

It was not to be supposed that the Governor, on taking up his residence in the Capital, would find either a castle or palace to receive him. Nor did he. The Duke de la Rochefoucauld-Liancourt, who visited Governor Simcoe in 1795, referring to the house occupied by the Governor, described it as a "small, miserable, wooden house, which was formerly occupied by the commissaries." There is every reason to believe that a torch was applied to the main building by the Americans in 1813.

The frame building still to be seen near the ruins of Fort George formed a portion of the original Navy Hall. Mrs. Simcoe's sketch of Navy Hall, made in 1794 from the deck of the government sloop *Mississagua*, then lying at the mouth of the Niagara River, shows two buildings forming Navy Hall, one a long building at right-angles to the river, the other parallel to the river. The long building at right-angles to the river is not there now. It was the main building, the one occupied by the Governor as his residence, and preponderance of tradition says was burnt by the Americans in 1813, though I have not been able to find any historical record of the fact.

Governor Simcoe, while he occupied Navy Hall, generally had on duty four men from Fort Niagara, opposite, which we must remember was still in possession of the British. The Queen's Rangers were quartered in Fort Niagara, but a guard from the regiment was regularly posted at Navy Hall.

Mr. Brymner, the archivist at Ottawa, says that it appears from the records there that on the 7th September, 1796, David Shank, Major-Captain Queen's Rangers commanding, forwarded to Captain Greene, Military Secretary, two estimates of the expense of removing the surplus ordnance stores to Quebec, one signed by Allan McLean, Assistant Commissary and Store-Keeper, and the other by Robert Pilkington, Lieutenant Royal Engineers, both dated "Navy Hall, 29th August, 1796." Major-Captain David Shank's letter, in sending in his estimates, was dated from " Navy Hall," and as he was an officer of the Queen's Rangers it is surmised that some portion of the regiment was at that post ; the main body of the regiment were no doubt quartered in Fort Niagara.

But to return to the Governor. We have seen that the Legislature was prorogued on the 15th October, 1792. The good men and true who had represented the people were now wending their way homewards, some by land, some by water. In those primitive days many an M.P. travelled to Niagara, to attend the sittings of the House, from his far-off home, on horseback, with saddle-bags in which was carried food for man and provender for horse on their way, frequently having to camp out in the woods, not unfrequently receiving good offices from friendly Indians, or, it may have been, from settlers of some distant clearing out on the hunt. Some of the Members of Parliament would return to their homes in bark canoes, skirting the margin of Lake Ontario, and by this route and the Saint Lawrence reaching their eastern homes.

The Governor himself had enough to occupy him

at Navy Hall in setting the machinery of government in motion. His Government was in the nature of a paternal government. He had great solicitude for the Indians, and as for the people, he regarded every man, woman and child in the province as under his special care or that of his officers. He could not dissociate himself from the idea that he was in some way at the head of a regiment, with himself and soldiers always on the *qui vive* and ready for active service.

The granting of land to settlers, and seeing that justice was done them, occupied much of his attention. To relieve himself of some of these responsibilities he appointed lieutenants of counties, the same as Lord Lieutenants in England, and committed to them the right of appointing magistrates and officers of of militia ; besides this a magistrate could, under his direction, assign in the King's name two hundred acres of land to every settler whom he knew to be worthy, and the surveyor of the district was to point out to the settler the land allotted to him. In appointing lieutenants of counties, the Governor evidently had in view the organization in time of a militia force for the defence of the country. The Governor, aware of the fact that the province was principally settled by United Empire Loyalists and Rangers, and that a greater influx of United Empire Loyalists was likely soon to take place, had confidence that he could have at hand a force sufficient for the protection of the country, and with the Indians as allies had hopes that in the event of the American Revolutionists becoming dissatisfied with their situation, a restoration of the British rule might be gained on the south side of the great lakes.

We cannot doubt that this was in the Governor's mind if we closely examine into his acts during the whole time he was Governor of the province. It must not be forgotten that during the whole of that period the posts of Detroit, Niagara and Michilimackinac were still in possession of the British, occupied by British troops, though within the territorial limits of the United States. The Americans had not carried out the treaty in its integrity, Might not then the English close up the Continental War, pay special attention to the colonies, and with accession of strength recover what had been lost through the weakness of England, in engaging in foreign war, and through the malign alliance of French and American Revolutionists in the work of the disintegration of the colonies? One great point gained would be in keeping the military posts well in hand, and in communication with one another. Directing his attention in this direction we find Governor Simcoe soon after the Christmas season of 1792, and while the year 1793 was yet young, making a trip through the woods from Niagara to the post of Detroit, and reviewing the troops (the 24th Regiment of Foot) at that place.   He set out on Monday, February 4th, 1793, accompanied by Captain Fitzgerald, Lieut. Smith, of the 5th Regiment, Lieut. Talbot, formerly of the Queen's Rangers, Gray, Givins and Major Littlehales in sleighs—the starting point Navy Hall, the destination Detroit, the post of the Straits.   This trip is a memorable one and it is interesting to read of it in the journal kept by Major Littlehales, the Governor's secretary, the details of which have been given to the public by Dr. Scadding in a pamphlet, with introduction and notes.   It would take up too much space to give all the particulars and incidents of the excursion, and yet there are some of the incidents which it would not be proper to omit. One of the incidents is, that on the fourth day out, *i.e.*, on the 7th February, the party arrived at Captain Brant's, at the Mohawk Village, about seventy miles from Niagara, or Newark.   On the arrival at the village the Indians hoisted their flags and trophies of war, and fired a *feu de joie*, in compliment to His Excellency, the representative of the King, their father.   We have seen that the Duke of Northumberland had by letter introduced Governor Simcoe to Brant—in Indian, " Thayendanegea."   The meeting with Brant at his own Mohawk village, on the Grand River, must have been a pleasant surprise to the Governor, and the firing of the *feu de joie* must have satisfied him that he might depend on the Mohawks, the faithful allies of England, in any well-conceived enterprise on the continent.

Captain Joseph Brant (Thayendanegea) was unquestionably the greatest chief of his day among the Indians. He was, in fact, a chief of chiefs. The Six Nation Indians, made up of the Mohawks, Senecas, Oneidas, Cayugas, Onondagas and Tuscaroras, formed a confederacy stronger than any other confederacy of Indians on the Continent of America, and Brant was their chief. The tribes separately had their own chief, but Brant was the chief of the united nations. Not only was he Chief of the Six Nations, but he had the respect of all the other tribes of the aborigines on the continent. He was directly or indirectly engaged in the wars between the United States and the Indians from 1789 to 1795, during which the bloody campaigns of Harmar, St. Clair and Wayne took place, and he took an important part in the affair of the North-Western posts, to which I have before referred, as retained by the British after the Treaty of Peace of 1783. He was an educated and civilized Indian, and is said to have been the son of Nickus Brant, a Mohawk chief, whose Indian name was Aroghyadagha; according to Sir William Johnson, but as given by his family, Tehowaghwengaraghkwiu. Brant was, in fact, of the noblest descent among his nation.

When but seventeen years of age, in 1759, he accompanied Sir William Johnson, the British Superintendent of Indians, during the Niagara Campaign of that year. This resulted in the capturing of Fort Niagara by Sir William, with his British troops and Indians, of whom Brant was one. The taking of this fort was a great blow to the French, as thereby they were cut off from their project of keeping up a line of fortified communications with Louisiana. Brant, it is said, behaved uncommonly well on this occasion. After the capture of the fort, and when a comparative lull in military campaigning took place, Sir William Johnson, anxious to improve the moral and social condition of his Mohawk neighbours—for, as is well known, Sir William had his hospitable residence in the beautiful valley of the Mohawk, in the State of New York— selected a number of young Mohawks, and sent them to the Moor Charity School, established at Lebanon, Connecticut, under the immediate direction of the Rev. Dr. Eleazer Wheelock, afterwards President of the Dartmouth College, of which, by its transfer, that school became the foundation. Among the youths thus selected was Thayendanegea. In 1762 the Rev. Charles Jeffrey, missionary to the Mohawks, took Thayendanegea as an interpreter. He was, however, shortly afterwards called out on the war path, as appears by the following paragraph in one of the

Rev. Mr. Kirkland's earliest reports to the Rev. Dr. Wheelock. Mr. Kirkland and Mr. Wheelock were missionaries and teachers among the Six Nations:
"Joseph Brant, a Mohawk Indian, and of a family of distinction in the nation, was educated by Mr. Wheelock, and was so well accomplished that the Rev. Charles Jeffrey Smith (a young gentleman, who out of love for Christ and the souls of men, devotes his life, and such a fortune as is sufficient to support himself and his interpreter, wholly to this glorious service) took him for his interpreter, when he went on his mission to the Mohawks, now three years ago; but the war breaking out at that time between the back Indians and the English, Mr. Smith was obliged to return; but Joseph tarried and went out with a company against the Indians, and was useful in the war, in which he behaved so much like the Christian and the soldier, that he gained great esteem. He now lives in a decent manner, and endeavours to teach his poor brethren the things of God, in which his own heart seems much engaged. His house is an asylum for the missionaries in that wilderness."

In the early part of the Revolutionary War the Mohawks were neutral. It was not long, however, before they were prevailed upon by Sir William Johnson and Brant to take up the hatchet against the Americans. They then left the Mohawk Valley and retired to Canada. Up to 1779 they lived quietly in Tryon County, Mohawk Valley, cultivating their ground or following the chase at their pleasure. When, however, the Mohawks did take up the hatchet they did it effectually, and were fast allies of the British till the end of the War of the Revolution. In 1780 a raid was made by the Indians under their gallant Captain Brant. In this raid the Mohawks made a prisoner of a certain Captain Jeremiah Snyder, and took him to Fort Niagara, and, from his observations while there, Captain Snyder afterwards. wrote a description of Fort Niagara as it was at that time, and also a description of Captain Brant himself. In his narrative Captain Snyder described Fort Niagara as a structure of considerable magnitude and great strength, enclosing a area of six or eight acres. Within the enclosure was a handsome dwelling house, for the residence of the Superintendent of the Indians. Describing Brant, Captain Snyder says : " He was a likely fellow, of a fierce aspect, tall and rather spare, well spoken, and apparently about forty years of age. He wore moccasins, elegantly trimmed with beads—leggings and breech cloth of superfine blue—short green coat, with two silver epaulets, and a small, laced, round hat. By his side hung an elegant silver-mounted cutlass, and his blanket of blue cloth, purposely dropped in the chair

on which he sat, to display his epaulets, was gor-
geously decorated with border of red."

The so-called border wars of the American
Revolution, which raged for several years, ending in
1783, were carried on principally to the north and
west of Albany. Brant was a prominent figure in
these wars. His allegiance to the British brought
on him the enmity of the American Revolutionists.
The consequence of this was, that no other section
or district of country in the United States, of the like
extent, suffered so greatly during the war as did that
of the Mohawks.

Brant's historian states : " The Mohawk Valley,
of all districts, was most frequently invaded and over-
run, and that too, by an enemy far more barbarous
than the native barbarians of the forest. Month
after month, for seven long years, were its towns
and villages, its humbler settlements and isolated
habitations, fallen upon by an untiring and relentless
enemy, until, at the close of the contest, the appearance of the whole district, was that of a wide-spread,
heart-sickening and universal desolation. In no other
section of the confederacy were so many campaigns
performed, so many battles fought, so many dwellings
burnt, or so many murders committed."

It was stated at a public meeting held at Fort
Plain in 1783 that the close of the war left only about

a third of the old population in the valley, and that in that third there were three hundred widows and two thousand orphaned children.

The treaty of peace with the United. States in 1783 did not by any means put an end to the Indian wars. In making that treaty the Indians were not consulted, nor were they parties to the treaty. In defining the boundaries of the country ceded to the United States no mention was made of the boundaries of the Indian lands. The Indians claimed all the territory west of the Ohio River, and yet they found that all that territory had passed from Great Britain into the hands of the Americans. The Indians denied that the Americans got any title to these lands ; they claimed that the lands were not the property of the British to give, but belonged to the native race of the country. It was matter of great concern to the Americans not to have an Indian war on their hands ; they consequently negotiated with the Indians, what they considered was a settlement of their claims. Captain Brant and his Mohawks stood aloof : they never could be got to desert Great Britain, though at times they had cause to complain of their treatment, especially the neglect of Britain to provide for them in the treaty of peace. It had been promised them that their case would be considered in any treaty entered into, and now they found themselves, deserted and left to their own resources. Remonstrance was made by Brant, and finally he secured for the Mohawks the reserve on the Bay of Quinté.

Although Brant was Chief of the Six Nations, he did not have all the tribes in hand. The majority of them were willing at times to treat with the United States and end the Indian wars raging over the whole western territory. The view Brant took of their action is pretty well shown in a letter he wrote in March, 1788, at his home on the Grand River, to the private secretary of ·Sir John Johnson. Referring in that letter to what was transpiring in the southern part of the United States, and the course followed by the Indians of that country, he said: "We have had no particular news here from the southward, only they are preparing to have another great council in that country early in the spring, and I am obliged to attend myself there. As for the Five Nations, most of them have sold themselves to the Devil—I mean the Yankeys. Whatever they do after this, it must be for the Yankeys, not for the Indians or the English. We must speak to them once more. We must, in the first place, get the Mohawks away from the Bay of Quinté. As soon as we can get them here we shall begin to argue to the Five Nations, and will show an example of getting together ourselves ; also we shall know who is for the Yankeys and who is not."

This letter shows that Brant was looked up to by the other Indian nations, besides the Five Nations of which he was Chief, as he proposed to attend the great council at the south, which was called to debate and consider all the questions at issue between the United States and all the tribes in regard to the boundary of the Indian lands.

More than one council of the Indians was called for the purpose of settling the boundary question if possible. The English were interested in having a settlement come to, and were appealed to by the Indians both of Canada and the United States to exercise their good offices to obtain for the natives the rights they claimed. In 1790 the confederated nations of the Chippewas, Pottawatamies, Hurons, Shawnees, Delawares, Ottawas, Tustans, and Six Nations, after a consultation at the foot of the Miami Rapids with Captain McKee, the Indian Agent at Detroit, deputed a representation of chiefs and warriors to visit Lord Dorchester, at Quebec, for the purpose of consultation, and also to ascertain whether any, and if any, what assistance might be expected from the British Government. Lord Dorchester's views were at that time pacific, as were also those of Captain Brant, provided always that the United States would establish the Ohio as the boundary and relinquish all claims of jurisdiction beyond that river.

During this year and in 1791-1792 Brant was constantly employed in negotiating for the establishment of peace between the Indians and the United States. He often attended councils, corresponded with the Government at Quebec, and with the Superintendent of Indian Affairs and his agents, and in every way endeavoured to promote peace, at the same time aiming at getting substantial justice for the Indians.

We will now return to Governor Simcoe, whom we left on the Indian trail with Brant on the Grand River

Governor Simcoe and party did not leave the Mohawk village, on the Grand River, till the 10th of February, 1793. When they set out Captain Brant and about twelve Indians accompanied them. On the 15th we find them at the Delaware Indian village, having walked on the ice of the La Tranche (Thames) for five or six miles. Here they were cordially received by the Delaware Chief. Major Littlehales, in his Journal, says : " Captain Brant being obliged to return to a council of the Six Nations, we stayed the whole day."

It is not stated where this council was to be held, but I suspect it was in Canada, perhaps in Captain Brant's house in the Mohawk village on the Grand River, as we find that on the return of the party from Detroit Captain Brant again met them to welcome their return.   On the 18th February Governor Simcoe and party arrived at a bend in the La Tranche (Thames) and were agreeably surprised to meet twelve or fourteen carioles coming to meet and conduct the Governor. He and his suite got into them, and at about four o'clock arrived at Dolson's, a well-known hospitable house in that part of the province.   In the vicinity of Dolson's there was a considerable settlement on both sides of the River Thames.   The land was well adapted for farming, and even at that time, behind the settlement on the south, was a range of spacious meadows.

From Dolson's the party went to the mouth of the river in carioles, about twelve miles, where they found the remains of a considerable town of the Chippewas, where, it was reported, a desperate battle had been fought between them and the Senecas, upon which occasion the latter were totally vanquished and abandoned their dominions to the conquerors.   Following the borders of Lake St. Clair, the party came to the north-east shore of the River Detroit, where they were saluted by a *feu-de-joie* from the Canadian militia, and soon after crossed the river in boats, meeting with floating ice.   Arriving on the opposite United States side of the river, they entered the garrison of Detroit, which was under arms to receive the Governor, and upon his landing a royal salute was fired.   Here the

Governor reviewed the 24th Regiment and examined the garrison, Fort Lenoult, and the rest of the works. Thus we have the Governor of the British Province of Upper Canada visiting a post within American or United States territory, and there reviewing a regiment of British troops! Why may not the Governor then have had some hopes that perhaps at no very distant time the whole of the territory of the United States would again become dependencies of the King of England?

The party, on the 25th February, start out from Detroit on their return to Niagara by pretty much the same route as they had travelled when going to the west. On the 28th they stopped at an old Missisaga hut, on the south side of the Thames, when, as Major Littlehales relates, "After taking some refreshment of salt pork and venison, they, as usual, sang 'God Save the King,' and went to rest." Thus were the woods and way places of Upper Canada resounding with the strains of the national anthem, joined 'in by the Governor of the province and his friends exploring its wilds in the then far west.

On the 2nd March the party struck the Thames at one end of a low, flat island, enveloped with shrubs and trees, where they walked over a rich meadow, and at its extremity came to the falls of the river. The Governor wished to examine this situation and its environs, and therefore remained there all day. He considered it a situation eminently suitable for the metropolis of all Canada. His reasons were its command of territory, internal situation, central position and facility of water communication by way of the Thames into Lakes St. Clair, Erie, Huron and Superior, navigable for boats to near its source, and for small craft probably to the Moravian settlement. To the northward by a short portage a way was had to the waters flowing into Lake Huron ; to the southeast by a carrying-place into Lake Ontario and so to the River St. Lawrence.. The soil was luxuriantly fertile, the land rich and capable of being easily cleared and put into a state of agriculture, and the climate was not inferior to that of any part of Ganada. It will be seen from all this that the modern London, capital of the Canadian County of Middlesex, was nearly chosen as the place for the capital of all Canada.

On the 6th March the party arrived again at the Mohawk village, the Indians having brought horses for the Governor and his suite to the end of the plains, near the Salt Lick Creek, in that region. In the evening all the Indians assembled and danced their customary dances, the war, calumet, buffalo and feather dances, etc. Most of His Excellency's suite, being equipped and dressed in imitation of the Indians, were adopted as chiefs.

The grant of the reserve on the Bay of Quinté is dated the 1st April, 1793, which clearly proves that Brant, ever on the alert to secure justice to the Mohawks, had prevailed on the Governor to apportion to them Crown lands as an additional reserve.

This trip of the Governor to Detroit and return was evidently made with the object of seeing how best communication between the two British posts of Niagara and Detroit could be secured. The Americans were threatening to attack Fort Niagara, and drive out the British troops. If they could succeed in this they would easily be able to reach Detroit by the way of Fort Erie and Lake Erie, and capture that post. This operation the Governor felt it to be his duty to forestall and prevent.

On his return from Detroit to Newark, under date of the 5th April, 1793, the Governor wrote to Major-General Alured Clarke, at Quebec, informing the Major-General that many American officers gave it as their opinion that Fort Niagara should be attacked ; and Detroit must then fall of course. In this letter the Governor further stated, " I hope by this autumn to show the fallacy of these officers' reasoning by opening a safe and expeditious communication to La Tranche." But on this subject, he adds, " I reserve myself until I have visited Toronto."

The Governor carrying out his project of visiting

Toronto, on the 2nd May, accompanied by several military gentlemen, set out in boats for Toronto, around the head of Lake Ontario past Burlington Bay. In the evening the government vessels, the *Caldwell* and *Buffalo* also sailed for Toronto. Another government vessel, the *Onondaga* was already there with its commander, Joseph Bouchette, engaged in the first survey of the harbour. Bouchette, in his " British Dominions in North America," has left on record an account of this survey, which I will transcribe : " It fell to my lot," he says, " to make the first survey of York Harbour in 1793. Lieut.-Governor the late General Simcoe, who then resided at Navy Hall, Niagara, having formed extensive plans for the improvement of the colony, had resolved upon laying the foundations of a provincial capital. I was at that time in the naval service of the lakes, and the survey of Toronto Harbour was entrusted by His Excellency to my performance. I still distinctly recollect the untamed aspect which the country exhibited when first I entered the beautiful basin, which thus became the scene of my early hydro-graphical operations. Dense and trackless forests lined the margin of the lake and reflected their inverted images on its glossy surface. The wandering savage had constructed his ephemeral habitation beneath their luxuriant foliage ; the group then consisted of two families of Mississagas, and the

bay and neighbouring marshes were the hitherto unin-
vaded haunts of immense coveys of wild fowl. Indeed,
they were so abundant as in some measure to annoy
us during the night."

The Governor and his suite returned to Navy
Hall on the 13th May. On the fourth day after his
return (17th May) he heard of the arrival at Queenston of Col. Picken and Mr. Randolph, Commissioners
from the United States, appointed to confer with the
Indian tribes of the west, with a view to peace and the
settlement of the boundary between the Indian nations
and the United States. General Lincoln, another of
the commissioners, had come from Philadelphia by way
of Albany, instead of taking the direct route across the
country followed by Randolph and Picken, and had
arrived at Oswego.

General Simcoe, as soon as he heard of the arrival
of the commissioners, Randolph and Picken, sent invi-
tations insisting that they should consider themselves
his guests during their stay in Canada. He treated
the commissioners with great hospitality, and at their
request sent a vessel to Oswego to receive General
Lincoln and the stores of the expedition. The conference that was intended to have been had with the
Indians was to have been at Sandusky, and was to
have been a great Council to settle all outstanding
differences between the Indians and the United States.

The Indians had been very wary, and so early in the year as February had invited the Six Nations to meet the other nations at the Miami Rapids so that they could confer between themselves before meeting the commissioners. The invitation of the tribes was couched in this quaint language: " Brothers,—We desire you to be strong, and rise immediately to meet us at the Miami Rapids, where we want the advice and assistance of our elder brethren in the great work which we are about. The Western Nation are all pre- pared, and in daily expectation of the arrival of our brothers, the Crees, Cherokees, and other Southern Nations who are on their legs to join us, agreeable to their promise. And we desire you will put the Seven Nations of Canada in mind of their promise last Fall, to be early on their legs to join us, and that you will bring' them in your hand."

On the invitation to attend this council at the Miami Rapids reaching Brant he determined to be present. When the United States commissioners reached Niagara, which was not till the 25th May, they were informed that Brant had set off for the west on the 5th May. The commissioners remained the guests of the Governor throughout May, June, and a part of July, as Brant and the deputation of Indians to this preliminary council held at the Miami Rapids did not return to Upper Canada till the 5th

July, and the commissioners waited there to hear the result.

The United ·States commissioners while staying with the Governor were enabled to see something of Indian life, occasionally . visiting some of the Indian towns in the neighbourhood. Through advices received by them from their own government they had got a false impression of the views entertained by Governor Simcoe in regard to his position with the Indians. They had been made believe that the Governor was advising the Indians, through Brant and otherwise, not to relinquish their lands to the United States. When the Governor came to know that such an imputation was cast on him it was promptly and satisfactorily disclaimed, and at the request of the commissioners several British officers were detailed to accompany them to the Indian Council. While the commissioners were at Niagara the second session of the Upper Canada Legislature was opened, on the 31st of May, by the Governor with a speech, in which he uttered the true patriotic sentiments he was known to enter-tain, and impressed upon the representatives of the people the duty of remodelling the militia. He did not fail to remind them of the value to be placed on the British Constitution as opposed to absolute mon-archy, arbitrary aristocracy, or tyrannical democracy. It may, without doing injustice in any direction, be suspected that in referring to other forms of government in contrast to his own and that of the people in Upper Canada, he was speaking to the United States commissioners as well as to the representatives of the people in parliament assembled.

This speech of the Governor in opening his second session of Parliament is much too loyal and forcible to be omitted. He thus addressed his faithful legislators :

" Honourable gentlemen of the Legislative Council and gentlemen of the Legislative Assembly—

" The persons who at present exercise the supreme authority in France having declared war against His Majesty, I think it proper to recommend to your early attention the new modelling of a Militia Bill which the more urgent business of the last session prevented you from accomplishing. I have the firmest reliance that it will be framed in a manner suitable to the principles of the British Constitution, so as to unite the interest and convenience of individuals, with an establishment necessary to the public protection.

" It is with great satisfaction I am able to communicate to you that the insidious attempts of those who envy the prosperity of the British nation, or are avowedly disaffected to the principles of its ` Constitution, have been completely counteracted and defeated by the wisdom of His Majesty's councils, and by the affectionate attachment and spirited resolves of all ranks and descriptions of His Majesty's subjects; and it is manifest that upon this important occasion Britons have acted with that unanmity and loyalty which might be expected from men who know how to estimate the vain assumption of innovators, and from the virtue, the wisdom, the struggles and experiences, of their ancestors inherit those civil and religious blessings which are derived under a free constitution, equally abhorrent of absolute monarchy, arbitrary aristocracy or tyrannical democracy.

"" The principles on which those who exercise authority over the French nation support the war, which, they have so unjustly begun, against His Majesty's allies cannot fail to call to your recollection how often it has been necessary for Great Britain to stand forth as the protector of the liberties of mankind, and we may entertain a pious confidence that under the guidance of the Almighty Giver of all victory, His Majesty's arms, directed to the security of His allies, will be ultimately crowned with success, and that it will be the felicity of the British Empire to maintain the independency of Europe against all modern aggressions upon those equitable principles which our ancestors so wisely contributed to accomplish. . . . .

" Honourable gentlemen and gentlemen,—I have to recommend to you to proceed in that laudable course of unanimity with which you have begun your legislative functions, and to continue all your consultations to advance the interests and happiness of this colony by making those provisions for the due support of public justice, for the encouragement of morality, and the punishment of crime, which are necessary to the existence of society.   In all these measures that may promote the real welfare of His Majesty's subjects in this country, which may tend to the most intimate union . with every part of the British Empire, you cannot fail of meeting His Majesty's paternal and beneficent approbation, and you may always be assured that my best endeavours will always be excited to forward the public prosperity, not only from the duty which I owe to the King, but from the most sincere attachment which I bear to the inhabitants of this province."

CHAPTER IX.

The Commissioners' Visit.

THE Second Session of the Parliament of the province was in its fifth day when the 4th June, the King's birthday had its place in the calendar. The King's birthday, in the early era of the province, was kept with great show of loyalty to the Crown. It was on this day that the annual training of the militia took place. The men would muster at a place indicated, when they would be put through their drill by some retired officer of the line, dress with eyes front, salute, fire a *feu de joie*, shout "God save the King," and the martial duties of the day being ended, the afternoon was devoted to canteen duty and refreshments. It was the amusement of the young to be present on training day to see, and possibly to criticize, the citizen soldiery. The men appeared on parade some in one dress, some in another, as uniformity was not in the least thought of. If some goodman had an old military coat he would don it for the occasion : if he had not he would appear in his best homespun and beaver hat, while the officers generally were in full dress, with their scarlet coats, large epaulets, and fierce look, ready to trample under foot the very demon of war should he be met in the path.

On the 4th of June, 1793, the garrison of Fort Niagara and Navy Hall did all honour to the day—a royal salute was fired from the big guns at the fort, and the royal standard run up at the military post and on the Governor's quarters at the Hall. The American commissioners were still the guests of the Governor, and have left their account of the way the Governor and his accomplished wife observed this day of days in honour of the King: "On the 4th June, the King's birthday was celebrated, on which occasion the Governor gave a *fete*, ending with a ball in the evening, which was attended by about twenty well-dressed and handsome ladies, and about three times that number of gentlemen. They danced from seven o'clock till eleven, when supper was announced and served in very pretty taste. The music and dancing were good, and everything was conducted with propriety. What excited the best feelings of the heart was the ease and affection with which the ladies met each other, although there were a number present whose mothers sprang from the aborigines of the country. They appeared as well dressed as the company in general, and intermixed with them in a measure which evinced at once the dignity of their own minds, and the good sense of the others. These ladies possessed great ingenuity and industry, and have great merit ; for the education they have received is owing principally to their own industry, as their father, Sir William Johnson, was dead, and the mother retained the manners and dress of her tribe."

The compliment paid by the commissioners to the beauty of the ladies at the ball was not undeserved. Even at that early period of the province the Canadian ladies had gained a reputation for beauty and comeliness. The daughters of Sir William Johnson and his Indian wife were educated ladies of refinement. Sir William Johnson was himself a most dignified man, of good circumstances as superintendent of Indian affairs, and took pride in giving his daughters all the advantages of civilized life. From the number of men at the ball, it may be inferred there were no wallflowers. The garrison of the fort, no doubt, furnished a good contingent of officers to dance with the ladies at the Governor's ball. Navy Hall, though not furnished with modern electric light, was in the full blaze of the light of women's eyes, and brilliant with men of war in their scarlet coats, whirling in the dance with the ladies of the Capital at the Governor's first ball.

The great chief Thayendanegea, the friend of the Governor, was not at this *fete* and ball but was engaged in conferring with the Indians of the west about the settlement of their boundary. A month afterwards, however, Brant arrived at Fort Erie, where he met the American commissioners. Brant brought with him from Miami a deputation of about fifty Indians from the North-Western tribes, attending the Council. Brant and the deputation were instructed by the Council to hold a conference with the commissioners in the presence of Governor Simcoe. An immediate interview between the deputation and the commissioners was arranged, at the request of the former, and a Shawanese chief, called Cat's Eyes, opened the conference, and said : " We are sent by the nations of Indians assembled at the Rapids of Miami to meet the commissioners of the United States. We are glad to see you here. It is the will of the great chief of those nations that our father, the Governor of this province, should be present and hear what we have to say to you."

It might seem strange that the Indians of the Western United States territory should send a deputation to a Canadian Governor to consult with him on a matter so foreign to his jurisdiction, as affairs of the Indians, in their relation to the new Republic. It only shows what confidence even the American aborigines of the west, no doubt inspired by Brant, had in the fairness and honesty of the Governor of Upper Canada. The commissioners having arrived at Navy Hall, the conference commenced, in the presence not only of the Governor, but also of a large number of the civil and military officers at the seat of government. The proceedings were opened, on the part of the western Indians, by Thayendanegea. There was much talk, but nothing was accomplished at the first conference. There was an adjournment, and the conference re-opened on the 9th July, when Brant, with the belt and strings of wampum, which had been presented by the commissioners, in his hands, made a spirited address to the English and Americans, after which he announced that he and the deputation were ready to proceed with them to Sandusky—"Where under the direction of the Great Spirit, we hope that we shall soon establish a peace on terms equally interesting and agreeable to all parties."

Captain Brant, the commissioners, and the deputation of Indians of the west started on their way to Miami, and arrived at the mouth of the Detroit River on the 21st July, where they were obliged to land —the British authorities at Detroit forbidding their approach further toward the place of meeting. On the 30th July a deputation of twenty Indians from the

Council at Miami had an audience with the commissioners on the subject of peace and the boundary. The deputation reminded the commissioners that many years before the Ohio was made the boundary, it was, they said, "settled by Sir William Johnson. This side is ours; we look upon it as our property." Captain Brant remained at the Council at Miami endeavouring to persuade the Indians to come to an understanding and make peace. The discussions were protracted, and no result being arrived at, Brant despatched a messenger with a letter to the Governor asking his good offices for the promotion of peace. His Excellency wrote to Brant in answer that he, Brant, well knew he had always both in private conversation and in public messages, endeavoured to impress a disposition and temper upon the Indians that might lead to the blessing of peace. Still he thought the Indians were the best judges as to the terms upon which a treaty of peace should be negotiated, and at their request he had directed the Indian agents to attend their Council, and explain to them any circumstances which they did not clearly understand. There was another circumstance which Governor Simcoe thought would render it improper for him to interfere. He said : " Since the Government of the United States have shown a disinclination to concur with the Indian nations, in requesting of His

Majesty for me to attend at Sandusky, as mediator, it would be highly improper and unreasonable in me to give an opinion relative to the proposed boundaries, with which I am not sufficiently acquainted, and which question I have studiously avoided entering into, as I am well aware of the jealousies entertained by·some of the subjects of the United States of the interference of the British Government, which has a natural and decided interest in the welfare of the Indian nations, and in the establishment of peace and permanent tranquillity. In this situation I am sure you will excuse me from giving you any advice, which, from my absence from the spot, cannot possibly arise from that perfect view and knowledge which so important a subject necessarily demands."

The commissioners of the United States were detained at the mouth of the Detroit River till about the middle of August, and up to this time they had neither been invited to attend the great Council at Miami, nor had they received despatches conveying intelligence whether there was to be peace or war between the United States and the confederacy of Indians of the west in the matter of the boundary.

Captain Brant and the Six Nations at the Council held fast together in their efforts to make peace to the last. All, however, was of no avail, as the other nations objected. The Council under date of 13th August,

1793, sent a despatch to the commissioners, with the ultimatum of the Council, which was to the effect that the Ohio River must be the boundary line between the United States and the Indian territories, and that all settlers—and they were many—who had taken up lands on the Indian side of the Ohio should be removed therefrom and the lands should be restored to the Indian nations. The commissioners could not agree to these terms. They accordingly wrote to the chiefs and warriors at the Rapids that "the negotiation was at an end." Thus ended this most important Council. There had been a great deal of talk, but nothing was accomplished. Unless another and more vigorous effort is made and concessions given there will be a renewal of hostilities between the settlers and the Indians, and much bloodshed on the plains.

During this period of the life of Governor Simcoe we seldom lose sight of Thayendanegea, one of the most prominent men of his day as Indian chief, negotiator, friend and ally of the Governor. His thorough knowledge of the Indians was of the greatest consequence in the mind of the Governor, who had ever before his mind the posts retained by the British in American territory surrounded by Indians who wished to be on friendly terms with the English: We must, however, return to Governor Simcoe himself, and see in what administrative and executive work he was engaged, while Brant was endeavouring to promote peace between the Americans and the Indians of the west and south.

The second session of the Parliament of Upper Canada closed on the 9th July, 1793. The Governor having now determined to make Toronto, on the north side of Lake Ontario, his capital, steps were taken preparatory to the contemplated removal of the government from Niagara. A few days before the end of the month of July the first division of the Queen's Rangers left Queenstown, and proceeded in batteaux round the head of Lake Ontario along the coast to Toronto. Shortly afterwards another division of the same regiment sailed in the King's vessels, the *Onondaga* and the *Caldwell*, for the same place. On the 30th July the Governor himself left Navy Hall, and embarked on board His Majesty's schooner, the *Missisaga*, which sailed immediately with a favourable wind for Toronto, with the remainder of the Queen's Rangers. We have the authority of Bouchette, who surveyed the harbour of Toronto, for saying that His Excellency, after landing on the north side of the lake, within the bounds of what is now Toronto, "inhabited during that summer, and through the winter following, a canvas house, which he imported expressly for the occasion; but frail as was its substance, it was rendered exceedingly comfortable, and soon became as distinguished for the social and urbane hospitality of its venerated and gracious host, as for the peculiarity of its structure."

The Governor literally pitched his tent in his future capital, on ground that had been trodden by the French and Indians when the territory was in possession of the French during their occupation of old Fort Toronto. The exact location of this old trading post of the French was where the Rouillé Monument now stands within the Exhibition grounds. In 1760 the site of this fort was visited and reported on by Major Rogers, an officer distinguished in the then late French War. It is not of the fort itself, however, we wish so much to know as of the surroundings. It is uncertain whether Governor Simcoe placed his new quarters in the woods or on cleared ground. In the report of Major Rogers, to which reference has been made, he stated that "the wood had been cleared away over an area of about three hundred acres immediately around it." It is more than probable that it was within this clearing that the Governor established his home in Toronto. It has come down to us traditionally that the exact spot where the canvas tent was pitched was where the old military hospital used to stand on the margin of the old Garrison Creek, just immediately north of the Northern Railway where it crosses the Creek. Dr. Scadding in his memorial volume, "Toronto Past and Present," has referred to the tent of the Governor thus : " It," he says, " must have been a pavilion of considerable dimensions, and was doubtless planted with considerable care by the soldiers and others. It was literally the prætorium of the camp ; the General's headquarters ; only, unlike the prætorium of old, it was movable and made of perishable materials."

This house-tent in which the Governor established his headquarters had a history. He had purchased it in England for the accommodation of himself and his family, when Captain Cook's effects were sold there. If that tent could speak it would perhaps have told us something of its owner Captain James Cook, one of England's most celebrated navigators ; how he was born near Whitby in Yorkshire, in the year 1727, and at an early age was put apprentice to a shopkeeper in a neighbouring village. His natural inclination not having been consulted on this occasion, he soon quitted the counter, and bound himself for nine years to the master of a vessel in the coal trade. At the breaking out of the war of 1755 he entered into the King's service on board the *Eagle*, at that time commanded by Captain Hamer, and afterwards by Sir Hugh Palliser, who soon discovered his merit, and introduced him on the quarterdeck. In the year 1758 we find him master of the *Northumberland*, the flag-ship of Lord Colville, who had then the command of the squadron stationed on the coast of America. At the siege of Quebec Sir Charles Saunders committed to his'charge the execution of services of the first importance in the naval department. He piloted the boats to the attack of Montmorency ; conducted the embarkation to the plains of Abraham ; examined the passage, and laid buoys for the security of the large ships in proceeding up the river. The courage and address with which he acquitted himself in these services, gained him the warm friendship of Lord Colville and Sir Hugh Palliser, and through them he secured a commission to survey the Gulf of St. Lawrence and the ·coasts of Newfoundland. In this employment he continued till the year 1767, when he was chosen by Sir Edward Hawke to command an expedition under the Royal Society to the South Seas for the purpose of observing the transit of Venus, and prosecuting discoveries in that part of the globe.

He made two voyages round the world, and was engaged in making his third voyage when unhappily he lost his life at the hands of those he wished to befriend.

On the 9th February, 1776, he received a commission to command his Majesty's ship *Resolution.* The ship was supplied with as much of every necessary article as could be conveniently stowed. The tent that Governor Simcoe set up in York as his movable house formed part of the equipment. At the time Captain Cook set out on his third voyage, in July, 1776, the Revolutionary War was looming up. Referring to the revolt and his own circumstances, and his leaving England on a voyage of discovery, in search of the north-west passage, by way of Behring's Strait, he says, in the journal of his voyage: "It could not but occur to us as a solemn and affecting circumstance, that, at the very instant of our departure upon a voyage, the object of which was to benefit Europe by making fresh discoveries in North America, there should be the unhappy necessity of employing others of His Majesty's ships, and of conveying numerous bodies of land forces, to secure the obedience of those parts of that continent which had been discovered and settled by our countrymen in the last century. On the 6th His Majesty's ships *Diamond*, *Ambuscade* and *Unicorn*, with a fleet of transports, consisting of sixty-two sail, bound for America, with the last division of the Hessian troops and some horse, were forced into the Sound with a strong north-west wind."

The Hessian troops here referred to are the same that were joined with the Queen's Rangers, and referred to in the chapters on the campaigns of Simcoe in the Revolutionary War.

While Captain Cook was actively employed in

seeking out new lands, Lieut.-Col. Simcoe and the Hessians were striving to stay the rebellion in America, so much deplored by the best minds in England and the loyal subjects of the Crown in all countries. A time came when Captain Cook, who had rendered eminent service in his voyages of dis-. covery, fell a victim to the passion and prejudice of the natives of Owhyhee (Hawaii). In January, 1779, he was directing a force that had landed from his ship at Karakakooa Bay to regain possession of a cutter that had been stolen by the islanders, when he was stabbed in the back by one of the natives. He was at the time giving orders to the men in the boats which had left the ship to assist him in his enterprise. The cruel stab given by the native caused him to fall on his face into the water. On seeing him fall the islanders set up a great shout, his body was immediately dragged on shore and surrounded by the enemy, who snatching the daggers out of each other's hands, showed a savage eagerness to have a share in his destruction. Thus fell this great commander after a life of honourable service in the cause of science —a life that did honour to the country of his birth.

I have incidentally mentioned the name of Major Rogers, and his visit to Toronto in 1760. The reader will naturally wish to know more of this officer, who took a very conspicuous part in the French and Indian

War of 1755-1760 ; in the old French War before the Revolution, and also commanded a corps called Rogers' Rangers. Major Rogers was the son of James Rogers, originally from Ireland, or of Irish descent, and one of the first settlers of Dumbarton, New Hampshire. He was born in Londonderry, New Hampshire, in 1727. When a boy, he became inured to all the hardships of frontier life. He was much among the Indians and became thoroughly familiarized with their ways and customs. When he arrived at manhood he was six feet in height, well proportioned, and had a reputation for strength, activity and endurance not equalled by any man of his time. In the French and Indian Wars he acquired a name and fame not eclipsed by any officer then distinguished. Governor Hill, of New Hampshire, in a letter written by him to General Robert Davis in 1842, thus wrote of him : " Major Rogers never resided in this State permanently after the commencement of the Revolutionary War. He was in the British service in Canada, after the close of the old French War, partly in a military and partly in a civil capacity. I consider him to have been one of the most talented men of the country—perhaps the best partizan officer this country ever produced. I believe him to have been the author of that perfect mode of attack and defence which enabled a hundred of the Rangers to do more service than a thousand of the British regulars, especially in the winter service of the old war of 1756. Such safety to troops on fatigue, amidst the severest seasons of a severe climate, was never before secured ; such certainty in the results, either on the advance or retreat, perhaps has never been realized by any other force than the Rangers, under the perfect arrangement and discipline invented by Rogers. I consider him to have been as great a man, in his peculiar sphere, as Napoleon Bonaparte, and for decision and firmness equal to Andrew Jackson."

This eulogy, coming from an American, though somewhat extravagant, gives a very fair account of the man as handed down to us in history. When Pontiac besieged Detroit in 1763 Major Rogers was sent with a body of troops to the relief of that garrison, and he assisted in the sortie from the fort at that time. Before this he had been most active in the campaigns entered upon by General Amherst in 1760, for the capture of Montreal, and which ended in the surrender, by Monsieur de Vaudreuil, to the British of the ancient Province of Quebec, upon which the French had set very high value, but which they were unable to hold. In describing the surrender, Major Rogers in his journal thus expresses himself : " Thus, at the end of the fifth campaign, Montreal and the whole country of Canada was given up, and became subject to the King of Great Britain ; a conquest perhaps of the greatest importance that is to be met with in the British annals, whether we consider the prodigious extent of country we are hereby made masters of, the vast addition it must make to trade and navigation, or the security it must afford to the northern provinces of America, particularly those flourishing ones of New England and New York, the irretrievable loss France sustains hereby, and the importance it must give the British Crown among the several States of Europe.   All this, I say, duly considered, will, perhaps in its consequences, render the year 1760 more glorious than any preceding."

After the capitulation of the French at Montreal, Major Rogers was commissioned by General Amherst to proceed with two companies of his Rangers in whale-boats from Montreal to Michilimackinac, and on the way to accept the surrender of Forts Niagara, Presque Isle (now Erie, Pa.) and Detroit, and when this work was completed to report to the Major-General at Albany, or wherever he might be.   In pursuance of this order Major Rogers embarked at Montreal on 13th September, 1760, with two hundred Rangers in fifteen whale boats, ascended the rapids of the St. Lawrence, and arrived at a place where stood the old Fort of Frontenac on the 23rd September.   From thence the Major, the Rangers and the whale·boats skirted the north shore of Lake Ontario till they reached the "River Toronto," having run "seventy miles"—thence they crossed over the lake to Fort Niagara, accepted the surrender of that fort, and then proceeded on their way, making the portage to Lake Erie, where they again embarked, continued their voyage to Detroit, having by the way accepted the surrender of Presque Isle. The Major, after some parleying, obtained the surrender of Detroit. In consequence of meeting floating ice in Lake Huron he was not able to reach Michilimackinac, which was not surrendered till the following year. This voyage of Major Rogers is a noticeable one, in showing the means taken at that day to carry troops up the rivers, rapids and lakes of the country, as well as recording the surrender of the last vestige of French power in Canada. After taking part in the relief of Detroit in 1763 he went to England and published two books, one his Journal and the other his Concise Account of North America. He remained in England till 1766, when he was appointed commandant at Michilimackinac, which after the conquest of Canada and surrender of the posts to the English, had become the most important military and trading post in the interior. As commandant of the post at Michilimackinac, Major Rogers was not a success. He thoroughly failed as an administrator. He was accused of entering into trade with the Indians ; of incurring expenses without authority, and drawing orders upon the government which went to protest for non-payment. He was charged also with a design to plunder the fort, and then to desert to the French. On these charges he was arrested, brought a prisoner to Montreal, and acquitted after investigation of the matters alleged against him. In 1769 he went to England. Shortly after this (according to his own account) he went to the Barbary States, and entering the service of the Dey of Algiers, fought in two battles while in his employment. On the breaking out of the Revolutionary War he returned to America in 1776, and was commissioned to the rank of Lieutenant-Colonel Commandant, to raise a partizan corps to be known as the Queen's Rangers. This was in truth the origin of the regiment, "The Queen's Rangers," afterwards commanded by Lieut.-Col. Simcoe. Rogers was not successful in this new venture. He was surprised by Americans near Long Island Sound in October, 1776, a portion of his command was captured and he himself narrowly escaped. He surrendered his command, went to England soon after this, and remained there till his death, which was in the year 1800.

We must now leave Major Rogers and return to the Governor in Toronto with his Queen's Rangers and other troops, besides the officials and civilians who had come over with him or followed after him from Niagara.

Going back to the opening of the Session of Parliament in the year 1793, we remember that the Governor in his address to that body specially referred to the "war which the French had so unjustly begun against His Majesty's allies." Now, after the Governor had pitched his tent in Toronto, intelligence reached him that the English on the Continent had contributed materially to a success over the French, in Flanders, on the 22nd May. This contingent of 10,000 men was under the Duke of York, the King's son. It may be mentioned in this place that the Governor, on his first visit to Toronto had determined that the old Indian name of Toronto, should be changed to that of York, in honour of the Duke of York. There is no official record of how the name came to be changed. It is sufficient to say that the Governor so ordered and it was done accordingly.

On the 26th August, 1793, the following order was issued from the Governor's headquarters :—

"YORK, UPPER CANADA,
"26th August, 1793.

"His Excellency the Lieut.-Governor having received information of the success of His Majesty's arms under His Royal Highness the Duke of York, by which Holland has been saved from the invasion of the French armies, and it appearing that the combined forces have been successful in dislodging their enemies from an entrenched camp supposed to be impregnable, from which the most important consequences may be expected, and in which arduous attempt the Duke of York and His Majesty's troops supported the national glory ; it is His Excellency's orders that on raising the Union Flag, at twelve o'clock to-morrow, a royal salute of twenty-one guns be fired, to be answered by the shipping in the harbour, in respect to His Royal Highness and in commemoration of the naming of this harbour from his English title, York.

" E. B. LITTLEHALES,

" *Major of Brigade.*"

The heading of this order " York," coupled with the firing of guns, the running up of the Union Flag at noon on the 27th August, 1793, were doubtless designed by the Governor, not only to express to the people his appreciation of the victory won by His Majesty's arms, under his son the Duke of York, but also to signify that the capital was no longer to go forward under the Indian name of Toronto ; but thereafter was to be called " York," in honour of the noble Duke.

The first meeting of the Executive Council, after the removal from Niagara, was held at the Garrison in the month of August, 1793.

On the 9th September, 1793, Mr., afterwards Col. Talbot, a member of the Governor's suite, in a letter to Col. McKee, Niagara, written from York, said to him : " There is a most magnificent city laid out here which is to be begun in the spring." From this it appears that after all the capital was only in embryo. There were no houses ; the population, such as it was, dwelling in tents in the wilderness, having for neighbours the Indians in their wigwams, and the wild animals of the forest.

Governor Simcoe, in selecting Toronto for the capital of the province, was no doubt influenced by the fact that it had a magnificent harbour, and was distant from the United States frontier. The Americans were threatening to attack Fort Niagara, which they held had no place within their territory as defined by the treaty of 1783. The Governor, always keeping in view the necessity of affording free and safe access to the capital for the fur traders of the west, in October, 1793, accompanied by a party of officers, explored the country between York and Lakes Simcoe and Huron. It was quickly seen by him that a road through this region would in the future be a most important highway between the two great Lakes,

Ontario and Huron. The Governor was never idle, but always intent on developing the resources and testing the capabilities of the province. When one looks back to the country as it was at that time, almost an impenetrable wilderness, but now a land of promise and fertile fields, too much credit cannot be given to the men who were the pioneers of our civilization: and at the head of them may be placed Governor Simcoe.

In the autumn of the year 1793 the Loyalists, many in poor circumstances, were flocking into the province from the United States. I find in the Smith papers an order of the 10th October, 1793, signed by the Governor's own hand, in which he says, " I approve of the issue of 138 rations to distressed Loyalists at the post of Niagara:" and on 25th October, 1793, Major Littlehales, then at York, writes Major Smith, at Niagara, that His Excellency Lieut.-Governor Simcoe had ordered him to communicate to Mr. Smith "that all the Loyalists under Mr. Wilson's superintendence have permission, if they please, to come to York by the first opportunity, also that whenever any Loyalists or persons who may have business with His Excellency at York are recommended by the Chief Justices he will be pleased to order them a passage in any of the King's vessels free of expense."

Again, there is another order made at York on October 28th, 1793, signed by Major Littlehales, in which he, by command of His Excellency, orders provisions to the value of £150 be issued from the government stores to one John Wilson, an American Loyalist, and several other families, in all forty-six persons, who had removed from the Province of New Brunswick to Upper Canada, but arriving late in the season were in want of assistance. Many orders of the like kind were made, during this and the following years.

PORTRAIT OF SIR GEORGE YONGE.

From an engraved portrait after Mather Brown, in the possession of the
Toronto Public Library.

CHAPTER X.

THE BUILDING OF FORT MIAMI.

HE season of 1794 commences with active operations being entered upon for opening the road from York to Lake Huron, projected by the Governor. The Government Surveyor, Augustus Jones, came over from Niagara to York in January, 1794, being sent for by the Governor to direct the operations. The Queen's Rangers were set to work felling the trees, and soon had, as it were, hewn out, a highway from York to Lake Huron—this highway is now Yonge Street, so called after Sir George Yonge, Secretary of War in 1791. We have seen in the last chapter that the Governor had personally gone over the ground, and now the work was accomplished. Surveyor-General Smith in 1799 thus described this highway to the north : "Yonge Street," he says, "is the direct communication from York to Lake Simcoe, opened during the administration of His Excellency Major-General Lieut.-Governor Simcoe, who having visited Lake Huron by Lake aux Claies (formerly also Ouenteronk or Sinion, and now named Lake Simcoe), and discovered the harbour of Penetanguishene (now Gloucester) to be fit for shipping, resolved on improving the communication from Lake Ontario to Lake Huron by this short route, thereby avoiding the passage of Lake Erie. This street has been opened in a direct line, and the road made by the troops of His Excellency's corps. It is thirty miles from York to Holland's River, at the Pine Fort, called Gwillimbury, where the road ends ; from thence you descend into Lake Simcoe, and having passed it, there are two passages into Lake Huron ; the one by the river Severn, which conveys the waters of Lake Simcoe into Gloucester Bay ; the other by a small portage, the continuation of Yonge Street, to a small lake, which also runs into Gloucester Bay. This communication affords many advantages. Merchandise from Montreal to Michilimackinac may be sent this way at ten or fifteen pounds less expense per ton, than by the route of the Grand or Ottawa Rivers, and the merchandise from New York to be sent up the North and Mohawk Rivers for the North-West trade, finding its way into Lake Ontario at Oswego (Fort Ontario), the advantage will certainly be felt of transporting goods from Oswego to York, and from thence across Yonge Street, and down the waters

of Lake Simcoe into Lake Huron, in preference of
sending it by Lake Erie." Here we have a true
traveller's guide to the fur regions of the great west.
Governor Simcoe's prescience in laying the foundation of a great city has been literally fulfilled ; no
less so his .laying out the pathway for trade to
the north.

The year of 1794 was not far advanced when the
Governor was called upon by the Governor-General,
Lord Dorchester, to execute a very important duty—a
duty which required him to enter the territory of the
United States, and there construct a fort for His
Majesty's government. This was a proceeding fraught
with a good deal of danger, and much opposition from
the American government. Lord Dorchester had in
the spring of this year, and for some time previous,
been in England, returning to Quebec in April. On
his arrival in Canada he gave directions to Governor
Simcoe to proceed to Miami, and there construct a
post, which he deemed necessary for the protection of
that country. Early in April Governor Simcoe
repaired over land to Detroit, and with a strong
detachment of troops proceeded to the foot of the
Miami Rapids, and commenced the erection of a
fortress at that place. This movement caused fresh
irritation among the American people, since the reten-
tion of this and other posts had been a continual

source of dissatisfaction.   The movement of Governor Simcoe into the Miami Country, and the erection of a fortress there, awakened the strongest feelings of indignation in the bosom of the President of the United States.

Mr. Jay was at that time the American minister at the Court of St. James, and the President gave vent to his feeling of indignation in a private letter to Mr. Jay : " Can that government " (the Government of Great Britain), asked the President in the letter, " or will it attempt, after this official act of one of their governors, to hold out ideas of friendly intercourse toward the United States, and suffer such conduct to pass with impunity.   This may be considered the most open and daring act of the British agents in America, though it is not the most hostile or cruel ; for there does not remain a doubt in the mind of any well-informed person in this country, not shut against conviction, that all the difficulties we encounter with the Indians—their hostilities, the murders of helpless women and innocent children along our frontiers, result from the agents of Great Britain in this country.   In vain is it then for its administration in Britain to disavow having given orders which will warrant such conduct, whilst their agents go unpunished.   Whilst we have a thousand corroborating circumstances, and indeed almost as many evidences, some of which cannot be brought forward, to know that they are seducing from our alliance, and endeavouring to remove over the line tribes that have hitherto been kept in peace and friendship with us at a heavy expense, and who have no cause of complaint, except pretended ones of their creating ; whilst they keep in a state of irritation the tribes who are hostile to us, and are instigating those who know little of us, or we of them, to unite in the war against us ; and whilst it is an undeniable fact that they are furnishing the whole with arms, ammunition, clothing, and even provisions, to carry on the war, I might go much further, and if they are not much belied, add men also in disguise."

The proceedings of Lord Dorchester, through the agency of Governor Simcoe, with respect to the construction of this fort at Miami, naturally impressed the Indians with the belief that now the British were going to enter on an active war with the Americans in defence of Indian rights. After the council held at Miami, which, as we have seen, resulted in the putting out of the council fire with no prospect of peace, General Chapin, the American Superintendent, and General Butler, the British-American Superintendent of Indians, met the Six Nations again in council on the 21st April to receive their reply to a communication which had been received from the American

Secretary of State, proposing the holding of another treaty at Venango. Captain Brant was at this meeting, and in eloquent terms addressed the Superintendents ; he was glad to meet General Chapin and General Butler sitting side by side, with the intent of hearing what the Six Nations had to say. He said : " We wish to do no business but what is open and above board." Then addressing the American Superintendent separately, he said : " It is not in our power to accept your invitation, to hold another treaty at Venango ; provided we were to go you would conduct the business as you think proper ; this has been the case at all the treaties held from time to time by your commissioners."

Again addressing the American Superintendent, he said : " Brother—we, the Six Nations, have been exerting ourselves to keep the peace since the conclusion of the war, we think it would be best for both parties. We advised the confederate nations to request a meeting about half way between us and the United States (at Sandusky) in order that such steps would be taken as would bring about a peace ; this request was then proposed by us, and refused by Governor St. Clair, one of your commissioners."

Again, and here we have the independence of the Indians stated in no doubtful language : " Brother !" Brant said, " Brother !—we are of the same opinion with the people of the United States; you consider yourselves as independent people; we are the original inhabitants of this country and sovereigns of the soil, and look upon ourselves as equally independent and free as any other nations. This country was given to us by the Great Spirit above; we wish to enjoy it, and have our passage along the lake within the line we have pointed out."

Brant went on to reiterate the desire the Indians had, and the great exertions they had made for a number of years to accomplish peace, without being able to obtain it. He then said, "Our patience is exhausted, and we are discouraged from persevering any longer. We therefore throw ourselves under the protection of the great Spirit above, who we hope will order all things for the best. We have told you our patience is worn out; but not so far but that we wish for peace, and whenever we hear that pleasing sound we shall pay attention to it."

We gather from this conference that the Six Nations, who really represented the other nations as well as themselves, were really desirous of peace on honourable terms, but not for peace at any price. They were still claiming the Ohio as their boundary, and evidently thought that the Americans were trying to drive a hard bargain with them. At previous treaty meetings and treaty making the Americans had conducted the business as they thought proper, without regard to the Indian interests or Indian claims.

The President, in his communication to Mr. Jay, had rather over-stated the disposition of the British in regard to a peace being come to between the Americans and the Indians. There was no doubt of the alliance between the Mohawks and the English. We see that Brant, chief of the Mohawks, plainly stated to the Superintendent that the Mohawks were desirous of peace. The English, too, were desirous of peace, but not at the sacrifice of the interests of the Indians of the continent. There can be no doubt, however, that the erection of the fort at Miami, by Governor Simcoe, inspired the traders, and the mixed multitude, constituting the refugees and parti-coloured inhabitants of Detroit, with the hopes of a coming Indian war. These traders and others were doubtless active in promoting hostilities, and very probably made promises to the credulous chiefs, as coming from Governor Simcoe, of which he himself was ignorant. Two Pottawattamies were taken prisoners on the 5th June by the troops of General Wayne operating in the west. These Indian prisoners had a story to tell which, if true, put things in a very bad light for the British. They represented, and intelligence to that effect was despatched to the interior tribes by. their chiefs, that Governor Simcoe was to march to their assistance with fifteen hundred men. He was giving them clothing and all necessary supplies, and "all the speeches received from him were red as blood. All the wampum and feathers were painted red."

The character of these stories may be best gathered from the entirely different tale told by several Shawanese prisoners soon after captured. They said: "They could not depend upon the British for effectual support; that they were always setting the Indians on like dogs after game, pressing them to go to war and kill the Americans, but did not help them."

In May of 1794 the Indians of the west had their hopes further raised by a deputation from the Spanish settlement on the Mississippi River visiting them and declaring that the Spanish Indians "were on their feet, grasping the tomahawk to strike them" (the Americans). Said they: "We will strike together. Children —you hear what these distant nations have said to us, so that we have nothing further to do but to put our designs into immediate execution, and forward this pipe to the three warlike nations, who have been so long struggling for their country, and who now sit at the Glaize. Tell them to smoke this pipe, and forward it to all the lake Indians and their northern brethren. Then nothing will be wanting to complete our general union from the rising to the setting of the sun, and all nations will be ready to add strength to the blow we are going to make."

The Spanish settlement deputation still further declared that the Creeks, Cherokees and Chickasaws had also charged them with a message, assuring them that their hearts were with the confederacy, and that eleven nations of the southern tribes were then on their feet, with the hatchet in their hand, ready to strike their common enemy.

The confederacy alluded to by the deputation was the confederacy of Indians. Brant was the master spirit of this confederacy. His ambition at one time was to be chief or generalissimo of all the confederated Indian nations of America, when he would have rivalled the great Pontiac, so celebrated in Indian annals.

The chiefs to whom these messages from the west and south were delivered at Miami Rapids, immediately convened a council composed of the Wyandots, Ottawas, Chippewas, Mingoes, Munseys, and Nantikokes, before whom the intelligence was repeated.

The Americans were alarmed at these evidences of determined hostilities on the part of the Indians. An Indian war was likely to occur, with confederated Americans on one side, and confederated Indians with a British contingent of some kind on the other. General Wayne, on the side of the Americans, was making the most vigorous preparations for opening the campaign. Besides this, the State of Pennsylvania claimed a district of country on the south shore of Lake Erie, including Presque Isle, under colour of a purchase from the Corn-planter. This tract of country the Indians also claimed as their property, and that the United States had no interest therein. A council was thereupon held at Buffalo Creek to take this and other subjects into consideration, the meetings of which were commenced on the 24th June. The determination of the council was to send a delegation of their chiefs into the disputed territory to request a removal of the intruders, and General Chapin, the American Superintendent, was solicited to accompany the deputation. He did so, but the mission was not successful. On the return of the delegation to Buffalo Creek, another council was held to receive the report. This convention was on the 4th July. The general boundary question was revived during the discussions, and an address from the council to the President was adopted and transmitted by General Chapin. In this address the Indians re-asserted their determination to insist on the Ohio boundary. Some idea of the force of character of the Indians, and the opinions they held in regard to their treatment by the Americans may be gathered from this address in which was contained, *inter alia*, the following paragraphs :—

" General Washington, attend :—What gives us room for the making of so many speeches is because you relate all the former deceptions that have been used.

" Brother—We are determined now as we were before that the line shall remain. We have fully considered on the boundary we have marked out. We know all that we have received from time to time, and, we think, if you establish this line (the Ohio) it will make us about even.

" Brother—If you do not determine with our request, we shall determine on something else, as we are a free people.

" Brother—We are determined to be a· free people. You know, General Washington, that we, the Six Nations have always been able to defend ourselves, and we are still determined to maintain our freedom."

Captain Brant was not present at the Buffalo Creek council, being engaged in the erection of a council house for his nation at Grand River. Brant was, however, a watchful observer of passing events and while others were deliberating in council and attempting to negotiate, he was preparing to contest the disputed Pennyslvania claim to the lands at Presque Isle by force of arms. On the 19th July, 1794, he addressed a letter to Col. Smith, for Governor Simcoe, in which referring to the Presque Isle business, he said, on the part of the Indians, that unless a favourable answer was given at the time limited, "it is our business to push those fellows hard, and, therefore, it is my intention to form my camp at Point Appineau, and I would esteem it a favour if His Excellency, the Lieut.-Governor, would lend me four or five batteaux. Should it so turn out, and should those fellows not go off, an expedition against those Yankees must of consequence take place. . . His Excellency has been so good as to furnish us with a hundred-weight of powder, and ball in proportion, which is now at Fort Erie ; but in the event of an attack upon the Le Bœuf people, I would wish, if consistent, that His Excellency would order a like quantity in addition to be at Fort Erie, in order to be in readiness ; likewise I would hope for a little assistance in provisions."

The projected expedition of the Six Nations to clear out the settlers at Presque Isle was relinquished, in consequence of the President of the United States interposing to prevent further encroachments by the Pennsylvanians in that quarter.

The Indians of the west, on the 30th June, made a raid for the purpose of capturing a large number of pack horses recently arrived at Fort Recovery—a fortress which had been thrown up by General Wayne on the site of the battle ground of a previous engagement between the Americans and the Indians, where General St. Clair suffered a defeat. The Indians now in their turn were defeated by the Americans, under Major McMahon, and were driven back with great slaughter.

As an evidence that Captain Brant was regarded as chief, chief adviser, counseller and friend of the Indians, it appears that, although he was not present at Fort Recovery, a despatch was on the 5th July sent to him from Detroit, giving full details of the engagement and the reverse suffered by the Indians.

We must now turn to Governor Simcoe and see what was engaging his attention while the land difficulties were causing bloodshed on the American side of the line. Just at this particular time he happened to have his own difficulties in settling the disputes of rival claimants, in regard to lands apportioned to settlers in his own province. Among the Smith manuscripts in the Free Library at Toronto there is a petition from D. W. Smith, Acting Surveyor-General to the Governor, dated 20th July, 1794, begging to be informed whether the lands on Burlington Bay "are yet to be reserved to the Abbé-des-Jardins and the French emigrants." The facts connected with this matter were that Governor Simcoe, who sympathized very much with the French Protestant emigrants who were driven out of France at the Revolution, had made an order that certain lands on Burlington Bay should be reserved for the Abbé-des-Jardins, and certain others for the French emigrants, and that the council had, by a subsequent order, and without consulting the Governor, directed "that those lands should no longer be reserved to the Abbé and French emigrants, but that the same should be assigned to the Messieurs McDonell. The Governor was by no means satisfied with this subsequent order, and very soon gave it its *quietus* by writing an order to the Surveyor-General at the foot of the petition : " You will be so good as to inform the Messrs. McDonnell that I consider all the promises made to them in respect to the lands as void, and as such shall order it to be laid before the council. I by no means intend to assign the parts exclusively to one family."

This order of the Governor shows how careful he was to guard against monopolies, and how ready also to assert his authority in over-ruling the council, if necessary, for the public good, and to maintain the faith of the Crown. Still, if at the present day a Lieut.-Governor were thus to over-rule his council he would put a strain on the Constitution that would endanger its existence, or his existence as Governor.

Governor Simcoe at this time was as much, if not more, concerned about matters abroad as with matters at home. We have seen that on the 5th July he had been advised by Brant of the defeat of the Indians at Fort Recovery by General Wayne, the Commander of the American army of the west. The letter of Brant further advised the Governor that General Wayne was only waiting for an augmentation of his force of three thousand militia from Kentucky; that he then intended to build a fort in the Indian country, another fort at the Glaize, and proceed from thence to attack the British fort at Detroit. This was unwelcome news to the Governor, as he well knew that the Americans were showing increased discontent at the continued occupation of the posts of Detroit, Miami, Oswego, Michilimackinac and other places within the bounds of the territory ceded to the United States by the Treaty of 1783. The richest and most extensive towns of the hostile Indians lay about the confluence of the Au Glaize and the Miamis of the lakes. The Miami Rapids were only fifty miles from Detroit. Shortly after the battle at Fort Recovery General Wayne took up his march in the direction of the Miami Rapids, and on the 8th August arrived within about thirty miles of the fort at the Rapids, which Governor Simcoe, acting under the directions of Lord Dorchester, had erected as we have seen. General Wayne, within thirty miles of the Rapids, and fortifying as he was doing, was likely to prove a dangerous enemy. Among the Indians he had acquired a greater reputation for boldness and courage than any other general opposed to them. He was so wary and careful in his movements, so like the Indians themselves in his mode of warfare, that they had given him the name of "The Black Snake," one of the most venomous of reptiles. The Indians had their own warrior chief, "Little Turtle" (a very prudent chief he was), and their chief "Blue Jacket," a Shawanese warrior of high character and influence: but they had come to the conclusion that "Black Snake" was a match for any of them. When General Wayne made his advance, and threw up works of defence within about thirty miles of the fort at Miami Rapids, the Indians collected to about the number of nearly two thousand in the immediate neighbourhood of the fort. The American Legion under Wayne was of about equal strength, exclusive of eleven hundred Kentuckians, under General Scott. There were a number of Indian villages around the fort at the Rapids, in fact the fort was in the heart of the Indian country, and General Wayne rightly conceived if he could break the back of the Indians at that place, he would have gone far in putting an end to the Indian War. The Indian chief, Little Turtle, got word of Wayne's rapid approach, intending to attack the Indians about the fort, and destroy their villages. Little Turtle was too wary a chief to be taken by surprise. He had his scouts out, and well arranged. As soon as he learned that Wayne was approaching he retired upon the fort at the rapids and prepared to give battle. Here was a dangerous position for all parties engaged. The British with their fort within American territory were surrounded by Indians who expected succour from the fort if the American troops should attack the tribes. The Indians were under cover of the fort if a conflict should take place there. The Americans could hardly be restrained from attacking the British fort if the Indians were receiving assistance from that quarter. Besides, among the Indians there were militia men and refugees from Detroit. These were then ready to take part with the Indians in the battle. The result of the battle, whichever way it went, might, and probably would, result in another war between Great Britain and America, which would be much to be deplored. Under these circumstances the American commander thought it his duty to make another attempt to come to terms with the Indians without the further shedding of blood. On the 12th August General Wayne sent a messenger with a letter and a flag to the camp of the Indians in close proximity to the British garrison at the Rapids. The messenger and letter were neither of them very cordially received in the Indian camp, but nevertheless, their arrival showed a pacific disposition on the part of the Americans. The Indians were not unwilling to treat, but, as was their custom, they required delay and deliberation before determining to lay down their arms. In reply to the letter of General Wayne, the messenger in his turn took a message from the Indians to the General, that if he would wait for ten days where he was, they then would treat with him, but if he advanced at an earlier day they would fight. The message did not, however, check the advance of the American force, and the General (Wayne) arrived in the vicinity of the rapids on the 18th August. On the 19th the force was occupied in reconnoitering the position of the Indians, and throwing up a fortification for the protection of the stores, which was very appropriately named " Fort Deposit." The enemy (the Indians) had taken post behind a thick wood, rendered almost inaccessible by a dense growth of underbrush and fallen timber, marking the track of a tornado, and almost under the guns of the fort (Miami), which had been erected by Governor Simcoe. The Americans advanced for the attack on the morning of the 20th. The Americans were very prompt in their movements, indeed such was the promptness of movement and the impetuosity of the charge, that the Indians, together with the Detroit militia and volunteers, were driven from all their coverts in a short ·space of time.   In the course of an hour the Indians were driven more than two miles.   The victory was complete and decisive. The forces of General Wayne were left in quiet possession of the field of battle.   General Van Rensellaer, who afterwards ˙commanded the Americans at the battle of Queenston Heights in the war of 1812, was in this battle under the fortification of Miami.   Major Campbell, of the British service,˙ was in command of the British garrison at Fort Miami.   Happily there was no conflict· between the British garrison and the American forces.   The battle was entirely one between the Indians, some militia and volunteers from Detroit, and General Wayne's army.   On the day after the engagement Major Campbell addressed a note to General Wayne, expressing his surprise at the appearance of an American force at a point almost within reach of our guns, and asking in what light he was to view such near approaches to the garrison, which he had the honour to command.   General Wayne replied, expressing surprise that a British fort should have been lately built within the limits of American territory, and˙ added, " Had it (the battle) continued until the Indians were driven under the influence of the fort and guns mentioned, they would not have much impeded the progress of the victorious army under his command, *as no such post was established at the commencement of the present war between the Indians and the United States."*

Major Campbell rejoined, complaining that men with arms in their hands were approaching within pistol shot of his works, where His Majesty's flag was flying, and threatened hostilities should such insults to that flag be continued. Upon this General Wayne addressed a letter to the British commander, disclaiming, as Major Campbell had previously done, any desire to resort to harsh measures ; but denouncing the erection of the fortress which had been erected by Governor Simcoe as the highest act of aggression towards the United States, and requiring him to desist from any further act of hostility, and to retire with his troops to the nearest British post occupied by British troops at the peace of 1783. To this requisition Major Campbell answered that he should not abandon the post at the summons of any power whatever, unless in compliance with orders from those under whom he served. He likewise warned the American commander not to approach within reach of his guns without expecting the consequences that would attend it. This correspondence between the British and American commanders clearly demonstrates that the war of the posts was now at its height. Here we have the extraordinary spectacle of the two nations who had signed a treaty of peace

only ten years before, on the brink of war again
about fortifications and posts which one of the parties
had within the lines of the other, and which should
have been given up to the Americans had everything
gone smoothly and had the treaty been observed in
good faith. But the fact was that the treaty had not
been faithfully observed by the Americans, and the
British retained the posts which were in their possession at the time of the treaty as a kind of hostage for
performance of the treaty. But then, what is to be said
of the construction of the new fort at the Rapids of the
Miami ? This fort had been constructed under the
instructions of the Governor-General of Canada—being
planted there it had to be defended. The history of the
matter would seem to be that the Indians claimed that
territory as belonging to them, and never ceded to the
United States by any party who had a right to surrender their lands without their consent. As we proceed with the narrative the truth of the case will appear
plainly. The only notice taken by General Wayne of
Major Campbell's warning not to approach within
reach of his guns was his immediately setting fire to
and destroying everything within view of the fort.
Among the property thus destroyed were barns and
fields of corn, above and below the fort, together with
the barns, stores and property of Colonel McKee
(the British Indian Agent), whom the Americans

accused of stimulating the war between the United States and the Indians. It will not be out of place to give some description of what the Indian country was: " The margins of those beautiful rivers, the Miamis of the lakes and the Au Glaize," wrote General Wayne, "appeared like one continued village for many miles, nor have I ever before beheld such immense fields of corn in any part of America, from Canada to Florida." Yet all were laid waste for twenty miles on each side of the river, and forts were erected to prevent the return of the Indians.

It has been supposed, and not without reason, that the Indians carried on their war with the Americans longer than they would have done, had they not supposed that in some way the English would come to their aid if too hard pressed. Certainly this was the view entertained by Captain Brant, who was not at all satisfied at the failure of the British to give support to the Indians at the battle in the Miami country. This appears from a letter written by Captain Brant to Sir John Johnson, son of Sir William Johnson, in 1797, wherein the Baronet was reminded of various wrongs alleged to have been suffered by the Indians at the hands even of the King's government: " In the first place," wrote the Mohawk chief to Sir John, " the Indians were engaged in a war to assist the English— then left in the lurch at the peace to fight alone until they could make peace for themselves. After frequently defeating the arms of the United States, so that they sent messengers to endeavour to get peace, the Indians were so advised as prevented them from listening to any terms, and hopes were given them of assistance. A fort was even built in their country, under pretence of giving refuge in case of necessity ; but when that time came the gates were shut against them as enemies. They were doubly injured by this, because they relied on it for support and were deceived. Was it not for this reliance of mutual support, their conduct would have been different. I imagine that your knowledge of these things, and judgment will point out to you the necessity of putting the line of conduct with the Indians on a more honourable footing, and come as nigh as possible to what it was in the time of your father."

Intelligence having reached Governor Simcoe of the disaster at Miami he, on the 28th August, 1794, communicated with Captain Brant, stating that he himself would proceed in the first vessel for the scene of action. It is a matter of history that the English not only retained these posts in the then far west, but posts within the boundaries of the State of New York. In the summer of the year 1794, an American officer, Captain Williamson, commenced a settlement on the Great Sodus Bay, about forty miles from Oswego.

Governor Simcoe promptly despatched Lieutenant Sheaffe to that place to demand by what authority such an establishment was forming, and that it should be immediately relinquished. General Simcoe, pursuant to his letter to Brant, and Brant himself, attended by one hundred and fifty of his warriors (Mohawks), proceeded to the Indian country in the vicinity of Miami Rapids in September. On the 30th September Governor Simcoe was at Fort Miami, as was also Captain Brant. The Indians had already made some advances to General Wayne toward a negotiation for peace.

Governor Simcoe and Brant invited the Indians to a council, to be held at the mouth of the Detroit River on the 10th October. This invitation was accepted, as was also an invitation from General Wayne, to attend a council, which a few of the chiefs accepted. The Indians were, by their representatives, in fact sitting in two councils at once, balancing chances, and preparing to make peace only in the event of finding little further encouragement to fight. At the council of the 10th October the Wyandot chief addressed Governor Simcoe as follows:

" Father—We request you to give your sentiments candidly. We have been these many years in wars and troubles. You have from time to time promised us your assistance. When is your promise to be fulfilled ?"

The Governor was somewhat embarrassed by this very direct question; still, conscious that every thing he had done had been sanctioned by higher authority, and knowing as he did know that the Indians had only been fighting for their rights, he made answer as follows:

" Children—Your question is very difficult to be answered. I will relate an ancient history, perhaps before any of you here were born. When I first came to this country I found it in possession of your fathers, the French. We soon became enemies of each other. In time, the Great Spirit above gave the conquest in our favour. We lived in this state for many years after. At last the Americans began to act independently, which caused a rupture between us. The contest lasted for a while; at last we made peace. From that period they have been encroaching upon your lands. I looked on as a spectator—never would say a word; they have even named the rivers that empty themselves into the Ohio.

" Children—I am still of the opinion that the Ohio is your right and title. I have given orders to the commandant at Fort Miami to fire on the Americans whenever they make their appearance again. I will go down to Quebec, and lay your grievances before the great man. From thence they will be forwarded to the King your Father. Next spring you will know the result of everything that you and I shall do."

The reply of Governor Simcoe to the chiefs in council had a pacific effect. Governor Simcoe was, however, so much impressed with the righteousness of the claim of the Indians to the territory west of the Mississippi, that he strongly advised the Indians not to make terms with the Americans but upon the basis of the Ohio boundary line. Brant was of the same opinion. He told the chiefs to keep good heart and be strong ; to do as their father (Simcoe) advised ; to return to their homes for the winter—that he would do the same, and come again in the spring with a stronger force. The Indians, following the advice of Governor Simcoe and the Mohawk chief, did return to their temporary homes, consisting of huts and tents in the neighbourhood of the fort at the Rapids. It looked as if the war between the Indians and Americans would be resumed in the spring, with the force of the Indians much augmented, and led by Brant, who claimed that he had always been successful in war. He further assured them that the English would, in the spring, come out from the fort, and join the Indians in attacking the enemy, when they would drive them back across the Ohio, and compel the restoration of their lands to the Indians. From the language used by Governor Simcoe in his address to the Council, there would seem to be no doubt that he was of opinion that on the state of the case being represented to Lord Dorchester he would, as Governor-General of Canada, furnish a large force to·join with the faithful allies, the Mohawks, in repelling the pretension of the Americans to the lands west of the Ohio.   Such was the position of affairs at the close of the year 1794.   The Indians were buoyed up with hopes, but still depressed by fear of General Wayne (Black Snake) and his army, which was still hovering around their settlements. When Governor Simcoe and Brant had left for their homes, many of the Indian warriors, who had come from a distance, were found to be re-crossing the Mississippi, declaring that it was useless to attempt to fight longer.   Even the Six Nations, the Mohawks excepted, were very much impressed with the uselessness of opposing Wayne and his victorious army. All this gave great concern to Captain Brant, who would have continued the war at all hazards.   Matters were shaping themselves, however, for peace, and before many months had passed negotiations were entered upon for more than one treaty arranging peace not only between Americans and Indians, but between the Americans and the British in regard to the posts within the territorial limits of the United States.

Governor Simcoe's vigorous championship of the cause of the Indians, and his vindication of his conduct in regard to the building of Fort Miami, no doubt had great effect in securing fair treatment for the Indians in making these treaties. The United States Secretary Randolph represented his conduct to Mr. Hammond, the British Secretary of the Legation in the United States, in such a way that he could not overlook his statement, and he replied to those representations in a despatch in which he vindicates his conduct in his usual forcible style. He wrote as follows :—

"Upper Canada, Navy Hall,

"October 20, 1794.

"Sir,—I was last night honoured with your Excellency's despatch, enclosing the copy of a letter to you from Mr. Randolph, Secretary of State, dated on the first of September ; and your answer, which intimates the intention of transmitting it to me by the first opportunity.

" It appears, upon the perusal of Mr. Randolph's letter, that I am called upon, by the respect due to his official position, publicly to state the misrepresentations of that gentleman ; and, on this consideration, not to pass them over in that silence which would otherwise best become the language and manner which the Secretary of State permits himself to make use of in his animadversion on my conduct.

" My having executed the order of His Majesty's Commander-in-Chief in North America, Lord Dorchester, in re-occupying a post upon the Miami River, within the limits of those maintained by the British forces at the peace in the year 1783, upon the principle of self-defence, against the approaches of an army which menaced the King's possessions, is what I presume Mr. Secretary Randolph terms 'Governor Simcoe's invasion.'

" The motives which led to this re-occupation furnish the true grounds for discussion, but the establishment of a military post, from its own nature, must have been so unquestionable as not to have required from you, Sir, on the part of Mr. Randolph, an avowal or a denial ; nor does it appear to me that he has introduced so public an event as a matter of doubt in itself, but solely as a ground-work for ushering into the world 'opinions' transmitted to the Executive Government of the United States, which, however respectable, are but 'opinions,' that British officers and British soldiers aided an attack made by the Indians on 'Fort Recovery.' Such an insinuation, Sir, introduced as subsidiary evidence of a fact, which required no proof, will undoubtedly on the undiscerning impress a belief that the British troops, instead of adhering to that principle of self-defence on which a post at the Miamis was re-established, were united in arms with the Indians in an attack upon a post held by the United States.

"As if to promote such a belief, Mr. Randolph proceeds to comment on the protest delivered to Mr. Williamson at the harbour of the Great Sodus. He terms this protest, which I transmitted in obedience to Lord Dorchester's orders, 'a mandate borne by Lieutenant Sheaffe under a military escort, and, in its tone, corresponding with the form of its delivery, being unequivocally of a military and hostile nature.'

" Mr. Randolph seems peculiarly anxious to consider every transaction of the King's Government, in its mode as well as in its substance, as hostility ; otherwise he could not but have seen in the protest delivered by Lieutenant Sheaffe to Mr. Williamson not a tone of hostility but a spirit of conciliation, explanatory of the first principle, on which the settlement in question is termed an aggression, the inexecution of the treaty on the part of the United States ; nor is it possible to conceive that less offensive language could be made use of, consistent with the formality necessary to substantiate a protest requiring the suspension of the exercise of a continental claim.

" Had Mr. Secretary Randolph made due enquiry, he would have found that the military escort consisted of an officer expressly sent to accompany Lieutenant Sheaffe, and seven persons to row the boat, soldiers most certainly, but unarmed, without military habiliments, and in the dress they wear for the purposes of fatigue.   It also might be presumed, from Lieutenant Sheaffe's letter, that he was personally acquainted with Captain Williamson, and in truth this circumstance was of some weight in the appointment.

" The general language and conduct of Mr. Williamson, particularly in the proposals of his speculation at the Sodus, have of late manifested a disposition so incompatible with those views of conciliation which are the true interests of Great Britain and the United States, that it became proper to select such a person as Mr. Sheaffe for this duty, being a gentleman of great discretion, incapable of any intemperate or uncivil conduct, and certainly not disqualified by being a lieutenant in His Majesty's service.

" Such, Sir, are the circumstances of this transaction, which Mr. Randolph is pleased to term my ' hostile views.'

" The following paragraphs do not seem to require

illustration. It can escape no person 'that what in the beginning of Mr. Randolph's letter to you he has stated as respectable 'opinions' transmitted to the Executive Government, is¹ no longer confined to 'opinions,' but the Secretary of State asserts, as a matter of fact, 'that the Governor of Upper Canada associated British with Indian force to assault our fort.'

"In respect to Mr. Randolph's assertion and his appeal to you, Sir, that 'it is grown into a maxim, that the affairs of the Indian, within the boundaries of any nation, exclusively belong to that nation,' I cannot admit so general and so novel an opinion as applicable either to the territory or boundary under consideration. I do not recognize its birth nor any state of its existence. It will be difficult for the Secretary of State to prove that it has governed the conduct of the United States, it is not to be found in the express provisions of the Treaty of Utrecht, it was never assumed by the British nation prior to that compact, it is incompatible with the national rights and injurious to the acknowledged independence of the Indian Americans.

"The British Government has not involved itself in disputes with the Indians by acting in so vague and indeterminate a manner. It has ever done justice to their natural rights ; nor has it violated the stipulations purposely made for their support and definition. In consequence of such a uniform conduct, Sir, the

Indians are constantly solicitous for the presence of
some of the King's officers or subjects at their public
meetings, and I have the most full persuasion that had
the United States concurred with the confederacy in
their request, that the King would extend his good
offices to the mediating power between them in the
present war; and that in consequence His Majesty
would have graciously permitted, as requested, me, or
with more obvious propriety, yourself, to have been
present at the late treaty.   In such a case, I am confident that peace would have been established on the
continent, to the satisfaction of the United States and
the comfort of the Indian nations, and scarcely in a
lesser degree to the benefit of His Majesty's subjects
in this province, who are materially interested that
their neighbours should on all sides flourish in wealth,
peace, and prosperity.

"As the close of the Secretary of State's letter
seems intended, through you, Sir, to 'apprize me
of the consequences of self-defence, should I not be
restrained by remonstrances,' the date of it cannot
possibly escape my notice; it bears that of the first
day of September, and on the 22nd of August General
Wayne advanced to the post at the Miamis, laid waste
the possessions of the King's subjects under its protection and summoned it to surrender.   It may be
proper to observe that so ill-informed was that officer

of the very principles on which he made his invasion, or 'self-defence,' that in his summons he requires 'the garrison to remove to the nearest post occupied by His Britannic Majesty's garrison in 1783.' Had this requisition been complied with, the garrison must have advanced up the Miami River into the Indian country beyond the post whose evacuation had been demanded. The discretion, good conduct and magnanimity of Major Campbell, the Commander of that garrison, prevented the commencement of war, and all its dreadful consequences.

"Upon the comparison of circumstances, the march of General Wayne, the date of Mr. Randolph's letter, I cannot but conjecture that it was written not to remonstrate against 'my excesses,' but to prepare the minds of men for whatever consequences might have arisen from the movement of General Wayne's army; and could the temperate forbearance of Major Campbell, and the event of the enterprize, have been foreseen (if I·may be permitted to revert to the object of this letter), I cannot but believe that I should have been spared the necessity of taking notice ·of Mr. Secretary Randolph's publication, or of controverting the assumptions of a gentleman for whom I have always entertained the most profound respect.

"To all, Sir, who knew my private sentiments, to yourself, Sir, who are acquainted with my public conduct, to His Majesty's ministers, and the other chief in command, who have approved of my strict adherence to their orders, and the consequent impartiality which I have maintained between the United States and the Indian Americans, any justification or exposition of my sentiments is unnecessary. Even Mr. Secretary Randolph has officially in -his possession sufficient proofs of good-will to the Government and people of the United States. They ought to have sheltered me from the imputations to which I have been exposed. I have ever shown the utmost inclination to cultivate the most perfect harmony between His Majesty's subjects and those of the United States, and have looked forward to an honourable termination of existing differences with the most anxious solicitude.

" I have the honour to be, etc.,

" J. G. SIMCOE."

In October, 1794, Col. Simcoe was promoted to the rank of Major-General. Before concluding his life we may be able to chronicle that he has had yet further promotion. But it will be in place to mention here that during the administration of the Government of Upper Canada by Governor Simcoe, the Duke of Kent, father of Her Majesty Queen Victoria, visited the Province. The Duke was at the time Prince Edward, and was stationed at Quebec with his regiment, having arrived a short time before the division of the Province of Quebec into the Provinces of Upper and Lower Canada. After the division of the province and the appointment of Lieut.-Colonel Simcoe as Lieut.-Governor, desiring to see Upper Canada the Duke set out from Quebec in a calêche, drawn by a French pony and accompanied by his suite. At Oswagatchie the royal party was met by a pleasure barge from Kingston, manned by seamen and military, accompanied by Captain Clark of the Naval Department at Kingston. From thence they were splendidly rowed to Kingston, where the King's schooner the *Mohawk*, Commodore Bouchette, Commander, received them. The Prince went on board and after a tedious passage reached Newark (Niagara), where he was received by the firing of guns. The Prince visited Niagara Falls, and on his return dined at Mr. Hamilton's, where he was much amused on witnessing a war dance by the Mohawks headed by Captain Brant (Thayen-danegea).

CHAPTER XI.

Establishing the Capital at York.

APPILY the year 1795 opens with improved prospects of peace. Before the year is over the Indian will have buried his tomahawk and the white man's rifle will have been consigned to its rack. The motto of Governor Simcoe was to be ready for War, but still to cultivate the blessings of Peace. He had a very difficult part to play with the Indians. The ever-loyal Mohawks had ever and always given him support. This was not always the case with the other Iroquois or Six Nations. More than one of these nations, and especially the Senecas, all in their tents or wigwams in the valley of the Mohawk and Genesee country, on the south side of Lake Ontario, would have made common cause with the Americans had it not been for the transcendent power and influence of Brant over the tribes. The southern Indians having left for their homes, the tribes of the Six Nations within the lines of the United States were

CANISE (Great Sail), NORTH AMERICAN INDIAN.

From an etching of a pen-and-ink drawing
by Mrs. Simcoe.

bent on making peace with the .United States. Both Brant and the Governor had thought and believed that this spring would see the Indians on the war path unless the Americans conceded to the Indians what they claimed.

Governor Simcoe during the winter of 1794-1795 was at York, engaged in projecting plans for the future of the place, its civil and military administration. A soldier himself, he could bivouac in his tent, but arrangements had to be made for public buildings for accommodation of officials and for the meeting of the Legislature.

Dr. Scadding tells us that in the previous spring materials could be seen lying about the nascent capital, few and far between, along as yet the scarcely distinguishable King Street ; hewn logs and beams, some scantling and plank, with bundles of cleft shingles, drawn there over the snow from the several shanties in the adjoining woods, where, by the help of broadaxe, adze and whip-saw, such objects were prepared ; a few heaps of lake shore stone or small surface boulders, to aid in foundations, and a few bricks for the chimneys, from a lonely kiln not far off, in the grounds probably of the expected " palace."

In July of 1794 the *Gazette*, the Government official paper, contained an advertisement : " WANTED, Carpenters for the public buildings to be erected at

York.   Applications to be made to John McGill, Esq.,
at York, or to Mr. Allan McNab, at Navy Hall."
Thus we see that the Government had only in part
been removed from Niagara, leaving much to be done
by the Governor in the winter of 1794-1795 to set the
wheels of progress and improvement in full motion.

The Governor himself was in the habit of spending
a portion of the summer at Navy Hall, the Provincial
Parliament continuing to assemble there until suitable
accommodation could be provided for them at York.
The town plot of York as defined at this time was a
small place indeed ; any of the country villages of the
province at the present time are larger than York at
the period of which we are writing.   The place was a
compact little parallelogram, bounded on the west by
George Street, on the east by Ontario Street, on the
north by Duchess Street, and on the south by Palace
Street, now Front Street.   Palace Street was so styled
because it was expected to lead to the Parliament
buildings, the only palace York was to have for some
time to come.

While on the subject of York, its foundation and
surroundings, we must not omit to mention that the
Governor recollecting the old land, its great houses,
castles and cathedrals, was determined to have a castle
of his own in the capital.   We have the authority of
Mr. Bouchette, for saying that His Excellency in the

winter of 1793-1794 made his headquarters at his tent or canvas house, planted as we have seen in the neighbourhood of the old fort at the entrance to the harbour, and far removed from the plot selected for the seat of Government. The canvas house was well enough for one Canadian winter, and the Governor made the most of it. He here entertained his friends with true English hospitality, the outcoming of an English heart. The hospitality of the Governor at Navy Hall had so impressed the Iroquois at Niagara that they gave him an Indian title expressive of his hospitality. This name was Deyonguhokrawen—" One whose door is always open."

We have seen that on the 10th July an advertisement appeared in the *Gazette* for carpenters for the public buildings to be erected at York. It was doubtless at this time that the Governor undertook also the erection of his castle on the banks of the Don. A description of this so-called castle will not be out of place. It was situated on a point of land jutting out and overlooking the beautiful valley of the Don, at the head, or nearly at the head, and to the east of the present Parliament Street and immediately north of the Necropolis. Parliament Street was cut out of the woods, first as a bridle-path to lead from the castle to the old Parliament Street near the old jail site, which was the site of the first Parliament buildings erected in York.

Dr. Scadding tells us in his "Toronto of Old" that
"Castle Frank (the Governor's castle or residence built
that year) was a rustic chateau or summer house, built
by Governor Simcoe in the midst of the woods, on the
brow of a steep and lofty bank, which overlooks the
vale of the Don. The construction of this edifice was
a mere *divertissement* while engaged in the grand work
of planting in a field, literally and entirely new, the
institutions of civilization. All the way from the site
of the town of York to the front of this building, a
narrow carriage road and convenient bridle-path had
been cut out by the soldiers and carefully graded.
Remains of this ancient engineering achievement are
still to be traced along the base of the hill below the
Necropolis and elsewhere. The brook—Castle Frank
Brook—a little way from where it enters the Don, was
spanned by a wooden bridge. Advantage being taken
of a narrow ridge, that opportunely had its commencing
point close by on the north side, the roadway here
began the ascent of the adjoining height. It then ran
slantingly up the hill side, along a cutting which is still
to be seen. The table land at the summit was finally
gained by utilizing another ridge. It then proceeded
along the level at the top for some distance through a
forest of lofty pines until the chateau itself was reached.
The cleared space where the building stood was not
many yards across. On each side of it, the ground

precipitously descended on the one hand to the Don, on the other to the bottom of the ravine where flowed the brook. Notwithstanding the elevation, the view was circumscribed, hillside and tableland being alike covered with trees of the finest growth. Castle Frank itself was an edifice of considerable dimensions, of an oblong shape ; its walls were composed of a number of rather small, carefully hewn logs of short lengths. The whole wore the hue which unpainted timber exposed to the weather especially assumes. At the gable end, in the direction of the roadway from the nascent capital, was the principal entrance, over which a rather imposing portico was formed by the projection of the whole roof, supported by four upright columns, reaching the whole height of the building and consisting of the stems of four good sized well-matched pines, with their deeply chapped, corrugated bark unremoved. The doors and shutters were all of double thickness, made of stout plank, running up and down on one side and crosswise on the other, and 'thickly studded over with the heads of stout nails. From the middle of the building rose a solitary, massive chimney stack."

Castle Frank was named by the Governor after his oldest son and heir, Frank Simcoe. The modern reader may think the title given to the house too big for the house itself. Still a house of this kind with "doors and shutters to the windows of double thickness" built of logs, and commandingly situated on a hill, might well, while it was the headquarters of a military Governor, have applied to it a title in imitation of the fortified places of England, when it, like Canada, was in its chrysalis and youthful state.

We have no particular record of the proceedings of the Government during the winter, but we may be assured that the Governor, who was never idle, was giving his attention to affairs of State. In the early summer of 1795 Mr. Hammond, the English Ambassador to the United States, advised the Governor that he was about to be visited by a distinguished nobleman from France, the Duke de la Rochefoucauld Liancourt. The reader will naturally enquire why a nobleman of France should at this time be found visiting Upper Canada. When we look at the time the reason is obvious. France was in the throes of revolution—a revolution in which the Duke was of the vanquished party, and of which, as one of the old nobility, he decidedly disapproved. He was therefore an involuntary exile from his native land, and his estates were confiscated. As he has said of himself, "By the Government of my country I am treated as a criminal or corrupt citizen ; severed from all I hold dear, I have been reduced to extreme inexpressible by Robespierre and the rest of the ruffians whom my countrymen have suffered to become their tyrants."

This was the man who was recommended to the

good offices of Governor Simcoe. We will see more of this French nobleman by-and-by. We find the Governor this year paying a visit to Brant at his home on the Grand River. The object of this visit was to ascertain the real wishes and condition of the Indians. There had been dissatisfaction expressed by the Mohawks at the intrusion of strangers, squatters on the lands that had been granted to Brant and his tribe by Governor Haldimand. The Provincial authorities had alleged that the Government had been deceived in regard to the location and value of the Indian reserves on the Grand River; that the Indians or their agents had represented that the tract lay a long distance from Niagara, and would not be approached by a white population for an age to come. Brant sternly denied the accusation in this regard, and declared that the Commander-in-Chief at the time of making the grant was thoroughly acquainted with the situation. The true history of this matter was that unprincipled land jobbers were settling on the reserve, setting up claims to the lands occupied by them, and endeavouring to influence the Government against the Indians; and making themselves altogether disagreeable, especially to the Mohawk chief.

The valley of the Grand River, in which the Mohawks had secured their reserve, was as fine and attractive a territory as any part of Upper Canada—

none more so. It was naturally, therefore, the envy of those who wished to possess themselves of lands at a nominal rate, even at the sacrifice of the Indians and their rights.

What with Indian difficulties, land difficulties, and all the various matters attendant upon opening up a new country, it can be well understood His Excellency was without many idle moments. In the month of June of this year he had to meet his Parliament, and now we may avail ourselves of the information afforded by the Duke de la Rochefoucauld Liancourt as to the ceremonies at the opening of this the fourth Session on the sixth day of July, 1795. Although the Governor had moved his headquarters to York, the Parliament, in consequence of there being no public building at York fit to receive them, was obliged to be assembled at Newark or Niagara as in previous sessions. The French Duke had entered the province at Fort Erie on the 20th June, 1795, and had been the guest of the Governor and hospitably entertained by him at Navy Hall from the time of his arriyal to the present time, the opening of the House. The Duke in his history of his travels in America has acknowledged the attention of the Governor in a manner which shows that he deeply felt his kindness. He says : " No sooner was the Governor informed of our arrival than he sent his Adjutant-General to invite us to dinner—having just alighted from his horse he could not come himself. We accepted his invitation, and shortly after dinner, he entreated us to remain with him, to sleep in his house, and consider ourselves as at home." This was true English hospitality ; so Navy Hall had the Duke as a guest, and during this time he was able to learn much of the Governor, his plans for opening up the country, and familiarize himself generally with all that was taking place in and around the capital. We learn from his narrative that the Governor's plan of settlement was to line the frontier with United Empire Loyalists and to place other applicants for lands in the back settlements. He was not averse to Americans from across the border coming into the province and taking up lands, but then he wished them to be settled behind the United Empire Loyalists, so that in case of war with the United States they would be but the rear guard of the army of defence. / He had ever before him the probability, or at least the possibility, of another war with the United States, in which according to his ideas Canada, fortified by the stout hearts and strong arms of the United Empire Loyalists in the front, with the Indians and settlers in the rear, would be able not only to hold her own, but to recover from the new Republic much, if not all, that she had lost during the Revolutionary War. Governor Simcoe was a true soldier and took a military view of everything. He never passed a hill or entered a bay but he thought of a fortress or a fleet. He directed the legislation of the Province in the direction of fully organizing the militia of the country. It is quite possible that had his views been carried out London and not York would have been the capital of the province. York was to him but a temporary abode. He apparently believed that London from its inland position was the proper place for the capital. The site where London stands we know had been visited by him ; he foresaw the day when the Indian posts would be given up ; and then it behoved the responsible authorities to have their principal city as far removed from the frontier as possible, with a dockyard, say at Chatham (named by him after the Chatham of England), for the building of wooden walls for the maritime service of the country.

We must not, however, dwell too long on military and maritime affairs, but proceed to the opening of the House of Assembly in July. At the opening of this Session of the House there were present but two of the members of the Legislative Council and five of the sixteen members of the Legislative Assembly. Nevertheless the House had to be opened at the appointed time, as within two days a year would have expired since the last Session, and the law required that at least one Session should be held each year.

The Governor opened the House with all the formalities and ceremony which in a major degree distinguished the opening of a Session of the House of Commons in England. The Duke de Liancourt says : " The whole retinue of the Governor consisted in a guard of fifty men of the garrison of the fort (Fort Niagara). Dressed in silk, he entered the hall with his hat on his head, attended by his adjutant and two secretaries. The two members of the Legislative Council gave, by their speaker, notice of it to the Assembly. Five members of the latter having appeared at the bar, the Governor delivered a speech modelled after that of the King, on the political affairs of Europe, on the treaty concluded with the United States, which he mentioned in expressions very favourable to the union, and on the peculiar concerns of Canada."

The Duke de la Rochefoucauld Liancourt had every opportunity of forming a true estimate of Governor Simcoe. As he was a foreigner and presumably impartial he ought to be a good and impartial witness of the merits or demerits of the Governor. He gives us to understand that he had an inveterate hatred against the United States. We suspect, however, that this was more in his manner than in reality. It perhaps might be said that he had an inveterate hatred of Frenchmen. And so he had in one way, and in the same way as in the case of the United States: he hated all people who were the enemies of England. Still in private life, officially and otherwise, he always was the courtly and dignified Governor of a province and the faithful servant of his King. His treatment of the American Commissioners, who were in a measure stranded in Canada, when in the province on Indian affairs, and his treatment of the exiled Duke show that his hostility either to Frenchmen or Americans was only political, and not in the least personal. De Liancourt says of him that he was "just, active, enlightened, brave, frank, and possesses the confidence of the country, of the troops, and of all those who join him in the administration of public affairs. To these he attends with the closest application; he preserves all the old friends of the King, and neglects no means to procure him new ones. He unites, in my judgment, all the qualities which his station requires to maintain the important possession of Canada, if it be possible that England can long retain it."

The Duke seems to have thought that England might lose Canada as she lost the United States. This, however, has not happened, and is not likely to happen if England continues to pursue a liberal policy towards the Dominion.

The Duke gives us to understand that the

Governor lived in a noble and hospitable manner—in a log house, it is true ; but it is the people that make a house, and not a house the people. The Governor, he says, was without pride, his record very enlightened, his character mild and obliging; that he discussed with much good sense on all subjects but his favourite topics were projects of war, which seemed to be the object of his leading passion.

This estimate, coming from a foreigner, must satisfy us that Governor Simcoe was just the man for the age and for the time and place he occupied.

The Duke de la Rochefoucauld Liancourt has given us a very good idea of the Governor's hospitality at Navy Hall. This hospitality was not a whit the less while making his temporary abode in the tent that had visited the South Seas, or while occupying Castle Frank in York. Here again we may quote Dr. Scadding. Referring to this he says : " We can picture to ourselves the cavalcade that was wont from time to time to be seen in the summers and autumns of 1794-1795 wending its way leisurely to the romantically situated chateau of Castle Frank, along the reaches and windings, the descents and ascents of the forest road, expressly cut out through the primitive woods as a means of access to it. First, mounted on a willing and well-favoured horse, as we will suppose, there would be General Simcoe himself, a soldierly person in the full vigour of life, advanced but little beyond his fortieth year, of youthful and stern, yet benevolent, aspect, as shewn by the medallion in marble on his monument in the cathedral at Exeter, revolving ever in his mind schemes for the development and defence of the new society which he was engaged in founding, a man just, active, enlightened, frank, as the French Duke de Liancourt described him in 1795. . . . . By the side of the soldier and statesman Governor, also on horseback, would be his gifted consort, small in person, 'handsome and amiable,' as the French Duke again speaks, 'fulfilling all the duties of the mother and wife with the most scrupulous exactness ; carrying the latter so far as to be of great assistance to her husband by her talent for drawing, the practice of which, in relation to maps and plans, enabled her to be extremely useful to the Governor.'" Dr. Scadding has added to the Duke's statement that the French traveller might have added "that her skill, facility and taste were attested by numerous sketch-books and portfolios of views of Canadian scenery in its primitive condition, taken by her hand, to be treasured up carefully and reverently by her immediate descendants, but unfortunately not accessible generally to Canadian students."

It is with pleasure I am able to say that through the kindness of Mr. Isadore Hellmuth, of London, On-

MONTREAL IN 1791.
From a drawing by Mrs. Simcoe.

tario, I have been enabled to give sketches from the portfolio of Mrs. Simcoe, referred to by Dr. Scadding as not generally accessible to Canadian students. At the time of writing I have the original sketches in my possession, for which I am indebted to Mr. Hellmuth. Mrs. Simcoe's maiden name is preserved in Canada by the designation borne by two townships, East and West "Gwillim"-bury, the former in the County of York, the latter in the County of Simcoe, named after the Governor. Mrs. Simcoe's father, at the time one of the aides-de-camp to General Wolfe, was killed at the taking of Quebec.

In the beginning of this chapter I expressed the hope that before concluding it I would be able to refer once more to that fruitful source of trouble in the early days of the Canadian Province of Upper Canada and the United States, which, commencing in the inner circle of the Indian war, extended to the posts and places occupied by the British garrisons in American territory; and in so referring would be able to say that not only was peace concluded between the Indians and Americans, but war was averted by another treaty between the English and Americans in regard of the garrisons to which I have referred. The victory of Wayne over the Indians at Miami was referred to in the last chapter. The Indians were not all agreed as to the propriety of continuing the war with the Americans.   On the 6th August, 1795, the opposing forces made a treaty, called the Treaty of Grenville, which concluded the long, expensive and destructive Indian war which had for so many years desolated the western frontier.   The boundary settled by this treaty was not altogether as satisfactory to the Indians as could have been wished and at one time hoped for, but, as the weaker power, the Indians had to submit.   Brant was not at all pleased with the treaty, and would not have submitted, or rather, I should say, have counselled (Brant himself never submitted) the Indians to submit to it had he not become convinced that the British themselves were about to give up the posts, and thus deprive the Indians of the succour they might have expected had these posts still remained in the possession of the English.   Brant, in one of his speeches, delivered long after the treaty was entered into, said : " The Indians, convinced by those in the Miami fort, and other circumstances, that they were mistaken in their expectations of any assistance from Great Britain, did not longer oppose the Americans with their wonted unanimity.   The consequence was that General Wayne, by the peaceable language he used to them, induced them to hold a treaty at his own headquarters, in which he concluded a peace entirely on his own terms."

Before the treaty between the Indians and Americans was signed, the two parties, the English and

Americans, had been negotiating for a settlement of the differences in regard to the posts, and it is not impossible that preliminaries had been arranged for a treaty. The settlement, however, was not finally made till the 19th November, 1795, when Mr. Jay, the American Minister to France, and Lord Grenville for the British, concluded a treaty by which the English were to evacuate the posts in 1796. And thus ended a controversy which might have ended in war. Happily the counsels of peace prevailed, and thus the whole continent was enabled to pursue its course of progress and development.

CHAPTER XII.

LAST DAYS IN CANADA.

OVERNOR SIMCOE, now in 1796, had gained all the experience necessary to successful rule in a new country. His career in Upper Canada had been closely watched by the British Government and by Lord Dorchester, the Governor-General and Commander-in-Chief in Canada, whose headquarters were at Quebec. Three years before this, viz., in 1793, the Island of St. Domingo, one of the West India Islands, had been taken possession of by the English troops from Jamaica. By the time the year 1796 was ushered in the British Government had been looking round for a man fitted to govern the natives in this island but recently occupied by British troops. Governor Simcoe's name would naturally attract the attention of the Government, but still he had work to do before he could, or would be willing to leave Canada for an island so hot and so black as St. Domingo. One work not yet altogether finished was the opening up of Yonge Street to the north of York. Augustus Jones, the surveyor, and his men had in a rough way laid out the road, but now, on the 4th day of January, 1796, he begins the formal survey of the route, and on the 4th February he reported to the Governor that the road was completed. The entry in the surveyor's journal is thus : "Went to the garrison York, and waited on His Excellency the Governor, and informed him that Yonge Street is opened from York to the Pine Fort Landing, Lake Simcoe."

The Fifth Session of Parliament, which the Governor called for this year, was a short but important one. The Parliament met at Newark, and was opened by Governor Simcoe on the 16th May and prorogued by him on the 3rd day of June. The most important Acts passed, and to which the Governor gave his assent, were an Act to amend certain parts of an Act intituled " An Act for the Regulation of Juries," and a certain other Act intituled " An Act to Establish a Superior Court of Civil and Criminal Jurisdiction and to Regulate the Court of Appeal," and another Act intituled " An Act for the Regulation of Certain Coins Current in the Province." There were in all only seven Acts passed during the session when the House was prorogued. After the prorogation of the House the Governor took up the subject of lands. In all new countries the land question is the one of all others that gives the most trouble, and causes the most anxiety to those charged with the administration of affairs.   We have seen that the Government had trouble with the Indians about their reservations.   Now those persons who had served the Government, as soldiers during the Revolutionary War or otherwise, were knocking at the Government door for their rightful grants of lands of the Crown.   The Governor's policy, as we have previously mentioned, was to settle the military class of settlers and United Empire Loyalists along the front of the country, so as to form a barrier against intruders on His Majesty's domain.

'Alexander Grant, who will be remembered as Commodore Grant of the Lakes during the War of 1812, and sometime Administrator of the Government, as we gather from the Smith papers, on the 6th June, 1796, petitioned the Governor "that he will be pleased to allot him out of his or his family lands 3,000 acres in the township in rear of York, upon the Humber ; one vacant front lot near Long Point, with 1,000 acres in the back concessions ; 1,000 acres near Point aux Pins, with two front lots on the lake ; 500 acres on the River Connon, including as much of that river as falls to the northward of the Indian reserve."

On this petition the Governor made this order : " It seems, agreeable to the general rule, proper that Mr. Grant's location should be confined to the Lake

Erie districts." Thus we see that the Governor adhered to his plan of allotting lands to those entitled to locations along the frontier. On the 20th June, 1796, a list of applicants for lands in the Townships of Walsingham, Charlotteville, Woodhouse, and Long Point Settlement was filed in the office of the Acting Surveyor-General Smith, and to this the Governor appended his sanction as follows : "Approved, and to be complied with as far as existing regulations in the opinion of Mr. Smith will admit." The names of the applicants for land in the townships above named, *i.e.*, Walsingham, Charlotteville, Woodhouse, and Long Point Settlement were persons well-known in the Province. They were : Ryerse, Maybee, Backhouse, Secord and others. In the case of Mrs. Maybee, a widow, about whose patent there was some delay in the department, the Governor was very peremptory in his order that, she being the widow of a Loyalist, prompt attention must be given to her application.

The fact that Mr. Jones reported to the Governor at the garrison at York shows that as soon as the Session at Newark was over the Governor had come to York, where he was residing for the summer, occasionally, with his friends, visiting Castle Frank. Dr. Scadding in the Semi-Centennial volume informs us that Castle Frank was never permanently occupied by the Governor or his family ; but pleasant excursions were repeatedly made to it while in course of erection and afterwards, in boats up the Don, as well as by the bridle road.

We mentioned in the previous chapter that Governor Simcoe, in 1795, visited Grand River, and had a conference with Brant as to the wishes of the Indians in regard to their lands. At this meeting Brant had delivered an elaborate speech containing the whole history of the grant, the circumstances under which it had been made, and the difficulties they had been called upon to encounter. The conference with Brant resulted in nothing more than a promise that the speech of Brant (Thayendanegea) should be forwarded to Lord Dorchester. As it was probable that the Governor would leave the province before the end of the year His Excellency confirmed such sales as had been previously made by the Indians, but difficulties arose on making the surveys, which once more disorganized everything. Another hearing took place before Mr. Claus, the Indian Agent, at Niagara, during this year, at which, in another written speech, the chief Brant gave a historical argument of this case. The speech of Brant clearly shows that it was the jobbers who stood between the Indians and the government as to the lands. Brant, in his speech, said : " I cannot help remarking that it appears to me that certain characters here, who stood behind the counter during the last

DISTANT VIEW OF NAVY HALL.

From a water-colour drawing in possession of Dr. Scadding, and made by Mrs. Simcoe, September 13th, 1794, on board H.M. sloop of war "Mississaga," then lying at the mouth of Niagara

war, and whom we knew nothing about, are now dictating to your great men concerning our lands. I should like to know what property these officious persons left behind them in their own country, or whether, through their loyalty, they ever lost any. I doubt it much. But 'tis well known that scarcely a man amongst us but what sacrificed more or less property by leaving our homes. I again repeat that if these officious persons have made the smallest sacrifice of property, then I think, they may in some measure be allowed to interfere, although it may be well known that personal interest prompts them to it, not the public good."

Captain Brant always said plainly what he meant. All of his speeches, of which I have quoted several, show this. He was always honest and dignified, and never let an opportunity pass of advocating the cause of the Indians whenever necessary to do so. He was perfectly fearless in all he did. It was always the same with him, whether in presence of king or commoner, he always maintained a manly bearing, and gave utterance to his thoughts without equivocation or embarrassment. In writing the history of Governor Simcoe I would not have given so much prominence to this chief were it not that he was not only a friend but fellow worker with Simcoe in all that concerned the welfare of the province, which he and his Mohawks had come into, under the determination under all hazards and under all circumstances to be and remain subjects of the Crown. The Mohawks are just as much entitled to be called United Empire Loyalists as were the most devoted of the adherents of the Crown during the American Revolution who had not a drop of Indian blood in their veins. As I may not mention the name of Thayendanegea again before concluding this work I wish to bear this testimony to his worth ; a worth which the country has recognized by erecting a beautiful monument to him in Brantford, so appropriately named after the great chief.

In reviewing the past, and what has been written of Governor Simcoe, I think it must be admitted that throughout his whole career, whether in camp, on the battle field or in the Senate he was entitled to a first rank among his fellows. When he came to Upper Canada as its Governor he came under an Imperial Law, which he knew had separated Upper Canada from Lower Canada, and that his lines were to be distinctively British. Mr. Pitt in his speech on the Canada Bill had fully explained the condition of things as they existed in the then Province of Quebec. He fondly hoped that by leaving the French of Lower Canada in the enjoyment of the old laws of Canada, as given to them by the Act of 1774, time and amalgamation with the English would in due course eradicate their fondness for the old system, and lead them to adopt in its entirety the English law as given to Upper Canada by the Act of 1791. He said that he agreed in thinking it extremely desirable that the inhabitants of Canada should be united, and led universally to prefer the English Constitution and the English law. Dividing the province he considered to be the most likely means to effect this purpose, since, by so doing, the French subjects would be sensible that the British Government had no intention of forcing the English laws upon them, and, therefore, they would, with more facility, look at the operation and effect of these laws, and probably in time adopt them from conviction.

The hard logic of events has proved that Mr. Pitt was much too sanguine in his hopes of amalgamating French with English in Lower Canada, either in people or laws. It is now nearly a hundred years since the Act of 1791 was passed. Up to this time the French have not looked at the operation and effect of the English laws (as given to Upper Canada) and adopted them from conviction. On the contrary, they still cling to their old idols, the laws of Canada as they existed in the reign of Louis XIV., before the spirit of progress and reform had permeated the French nation.

On the 3rd December, 1796, Governor, then Major-General Simcoe, was appointed Civil Governor of St. Domingo and Commander-in-Chief, in the room of Sir Adam Williamson. At the same time as he had this distinction conferred upon him he was appointed to the local rank of Lieutenant-General. These appointments necessitated his leaving Canada.

The *Gazette* of September 11th, 1796, contained a proclamation from Peter Russell announcing that "His Most Gracious Majesty has been pleased to grant his royal leave of absence to His Excellency Major-General Simcoe, and that subsequently the government, *pro tem.*, had devolved on himself. Mr. Russell had been senior member of the Executive Council, and, as was the custom of the time, became administrator of the government during the Governor's absence. It will be seen from the proclamation he issued on assuming the government, that Governor Simcoe had not been recalled but had been given leave of absence. When the new administrator issued his proclamation he was living in Niagara. The *Gazette* of November 4th, 1796, still published at Niagara, announced, "Yesterday (November 3rd) His Honour, the President of the province, and family sailed in the *Mohawk* for York. He was saluted with a discharge of cannon at Fort George, which was answered by three cheers from on board." It appears from this notice that the old historic Fort George had, at this time, come into being.

There was at this time a navy on the waters of Ontario, called the Navy of the Lake, which was really a branch of the Royal Navy, manned by seamen from the service of the Royal Navy on the Atlantic. Rochefoucauld de Liancourt, the French Count, with whom we met in the last chapter, has fortunately left us an account of what this branch of the Royal Navy was composed in 1795, and I do not know that it had been augmented by the time President Russell succeeded to the government in 1796. Rochefoucauld wrote : " The Royal Navy is not very formidable in this place ; six vessels compose the whole naval force, two of which are small gun-boats, which we saw at Niagara, and which are stationed at York. Two small schooners of twelve guns, viz., the *Onondaga*, in which we took our passage, and the *Mohawk*, which is just finished ; a small yacht of eight tons, mounting six guns, as the two schooners, which have lately been taken into dock to be repaired, form the rest of it." The Count in another part of his account wrote : "Two gun-boats, which are destined by Governor Simcoe to serve only in time of war, are at present on the stocks."

Captain Bouchette commanded the naval force on Lake Ontario, and was at the head of all the marine establishments. De Liancourt tells us that Governor Simcoe intended to make York the centre of the naval force on Lake Ontario ; that in 1795 there were four gun-boats on the lake, and that it was the Governor's intention to build ten smaller gun-boats on Lake Ontario and' ten on Lake Erie. It is to be regretted that Governor Simcoe did not remain longer Governor of the province, as in that case the naval armament of the lakes would have been kept up, and the province been able to give a better account of herself on the water than was shown in the war of 1812. So little did the British Government know of the capability of the province in the matter of furnishing war vessels for the lakes, that in 1812 the Admiralty sent out the frame-work, blocks, etc., of the *Psyche* frigate, which could have been procured on the spot in a tenth of the time, and at a twentieth part of the expense. The Admiralty were as ignorant of the quality of the water of the Lake, and evidently thought the salt water of the Atlantic or some sea was the fountain of supply to Lake Ontario, as at the same time they sent out the frame-work and blocks of the *Psyche* they furnished to each ship of war on the lake a full supply of water casks, with an apparatus for distilling sea water.

Canada took the lead in building the early vessels upon the lakes. The first American ship that navigated Lake Erie was purchased from the British in 1796. She was called the *Detroit.* The first vessel built by the Americans for the lakes was constructed in 1797. The first Canadian merchant vessel built upon Lake Ontario was by Francis Crooks, brother of the Hon. James Crooks. It was built to the east of the present United States Fort, at the mouth of the Niagara River in 1792, and was called the *York*. In 1800 a schooner of about seventy-five or one hundred tons, was brought to Clifton, and during the winter of 1801 she crossed by the portage road on immense runners to Queenstown, where she again found her native element in the Niagara river. Dr. Scadding tells us that she was in 1801 lost in bringing a cargo to Niagara, with all on board.

The subject of ships and shipping reminds us that, in President Russell's time, 1796-1800, the channel of trade in the province was more with Albany than with Montreal or Quebec. There were two reasons for this. In the first place, many, if not most, of the settlers who came into the province from the United States at this period of the province's history came by way of Albany and Western New York. The second reason was that the obstructions of the rapids of the St. Lawrence made it difficult to carry on trade with Montreal with profit or advantage. The consequence of a trade springing up between New York, Albany, and Upper Canada was that the province made rapid strides in its material growth and

development.   Posts of customs were established at
the frontier towns of Cornwall, Brockville, Kingston,
York, Niagara and Amherstburg.   Goods imported
into these towns from the United States found a
ready market with the country people, and at good
prices.   Commodities were exchanged between the
Republicans on the south of the St. Lawrence and
the lakes, with the John Bulls on the north side of
the river and the blue waters of Ontario, by which the
Canadians profited, and amassed considerable wealth.
Besides this, the tide of emigration after the Irish
trouble of 1798 set in in great volume, giving to the
country just the kind of settlers she wanted, to clear
her forests, build her roads and till her soil.   The
immigrants generally brought some means with them,
which. speedily found its way into the pockets of the
thrifty Canadian.   The construction of good roads
in the province was just as necessary as trade for the
full and complete development of the resources of the
country.   People lived wide apart ; the mills and shops
were at'a great distance from the homes of the settlers,
and without passable roads it was impossible to carry
on successful business of any kind.   Governor Simcoe
had been a great promoter of road making.   We have
in a previous chapter seen what care he took to have
a road opened up to the north of York; how his
Rangers were employed in hewing out for the people

a road in the wilderness. Governor Simcoe had intended to have a grand military road from one end of the province to the other. This he lined out, and gave it the name of Dundas Street. Had he remained in the province his intentions would no doubt have been carried out. In his time a small portion of the road was constructed, and settlers located here and there along the proposed road, who built houses with the expectation that the great thoroughfare would shortly be opened up. In this, however, they were doomed to disappointment, the departure of Governor Simcoe, and the fact that his successor, President Russell, was more intent on acquiring land for himself than making roads for the people, for a considerable time kept back the improvement of the country. The people of York were more fortunate in the road-making business than the inhabitants of some other parts of the province. In 1798, during the reign of President Russell, an American gentleman, named Asa Danforth, came into Canada, and made a contract with the Upper Canada Government to open a road from Kingston through Ancaster, at the head of Lake Ontario, which road he completed. The work was commenced in 1798, and finished in three years' time. This road passed through Prince Edward County by Wellington. For many years the main road was called the Danforth Road. I have said that President Russell was more concerned in acquiring land than building roads. It was notorious that during his administration large tracts of land were acquired by private individuals and government officials at a nominal price. Mr. President gained such a notoriety in this way that it got to be a common saying of those who were concerning themselves about land matters and the acquisition of territorial wealth, that there were many deeds about in which the conveyance ran : " I, Peter Russell, convey to you, Peter Russell." There may have been some truth in this, but it was certainly the case that the management of land grants was not exercised with the same circumspection as in Governor Simcoe's time. There was a large · number of land speculators—land jobbers they were called at this time—swarming in the government offices, very much to the injury of the country, but of profit to themselves. However, land-jobbing was not peculiar to Canada ; it had been said that "General Washington was not only a surveyor but an extensive land jobber, and thereby increased immensely his private fortune."

We will pass on now from the land speculator to the matrimonial speculator, and see what was being done in President Russell's time to faciliate the marriage relation. Before Peter Russell became head of the government none but ministers of the Church of England were permitted to perform the marriage ceremony. This was felt to be a great evil as not only inconveniencing those who were desirous of entering the holy bonds of matrimony, but retarding the growth of the country. In the year 1798, Peter Russell being President, an Act was passed to extend the provisions of a previous Act of 1793 (which had been passed to confirm certain invalid marriages) enacting "That it should be lawful for the minister of any congregation or religious community of persons professing to be members of the Church of Scotland, or Lutherans, or Calvinists to marry according to the rites of such Church," and it was necessary that one of the persons to be married should have been a member of the particular Church six months before the marriage. The clergyman must have been regularly ordained, and was to appear before six magistrates at quarter sessions, with at least seven members of his congregation, to prove his office, or take the oath of allegiance ; and then, if the dignitaries thought it expedient, they might grant him a certificate that he was a settled minister, and, therefore, could marry, having published the intended marriage upon three Sundays previous. Truly our forefathers were surrounded with many difficulties before they could enter upon the marriage state. No doubt this law was a boon at the time, but a very poor one at that. It was not till the year 1831 that the facility of marriage was enlarged, and the right of performing the ceremony conferred upon the Presbyterians, Congregationalists, Baptists, Independents, Methodists, Mennonists, Tunkers, or Moravians, in like manner as it had been previously conferred on ministers of the Church of Scotland.

Before concluding with President Russell and his reign I must make some reference to that most important subject, the militia service of the province. When Major-General Simcoe was Governor the province had been divided into districts and counties. The sub-division of counties was purely military, and related merely to the enlisting, completing and assembling of the militia. The militia of each county were assembled once a year in each county, and were inspected by the captains of companies at least twice a year. Every male inhabitant from the age of sixteen to fifty was considered a militiaman. There has not been preserved sufficient data on which to base a statement as to the enrolment or number of the militia before Russell's time. But in 1793 we have evidence that at that time there were Lieutenants of counties, the same as Lords Lieutenant of counties in England. I know that as late as 1804 there were such Lieutenants. My maternal grandfather's brother, Colonel James Breakenridge, was then Lieutenant of the County of Leeds.

On the 29th November, 179⅗, John Ferguson, of Kingston, wrote to William Bell, of the Mohawk village, in the County of Hastings, as follows: "Having been appointed Lieutenant of the County of Hastings, and being ordered to enrol the militia without delay, I must request you will immediately proceed with the enclosed notices and cause them to be put up as requested. This is the beginning of your duty, as I have recommended you to be Adjutant, as well as Captain of a company, and I have the satisfaction of telling you that the President has assured me that he will approve of my appointments." In a separate communication, Lieutenant Ferguson authorized Captain Bell "to give notice to the inhabitants to attend a meeting of Lieutenancy on Saturday, the 18th of December next, at ten o'clock, at the house occupied by David Burns, on lot 35, in the 10th Concession of Sidney, for the purpose of enrolment." Ferguson again writing on the 22nd February, 1799, says: "It appears from the President's letter that there is something brewing to the westward." On the 25th of February, 1799, Ferguson writes to Adjutant Bell to require the officers commanding companies "to cause the volunteers and drafts in their respective companies to assemble, with such arms as they have, at the house of Ferguson, on the Point of Sidney, lot 23, to be made acquainted with the purport of a letter

received from the Hon. Peter Russell, President."
Col. Ferguson, writing again on February 26th to
Captain Bell, informs him that the President has
been pleased to approve of the appointments made,
and that he must meet him at Sidney, 5th March, to
receive his commission. On the 1st of March he
further writes : " There is some appearance of the
militia being embodied next spring, and that Captain
Bell is appointed to take command of the detachment
should such an event take place." In a communication
dated 10th March, 1799, Col. Ferguson refers Captain
Bell to an enclosure from President Russell, giving
directions as to teaching the volunteers and drafts,
" who are to assemble at Wallbridge every other
Saturday for platoon exercise, etc. The following is a
list of officers of the Hastings militia, as approved by
His Honour, the President, with the dates of their
commission : John Ferguson, Lieutenant of County ;
date of commission, 1798. The following officers were
commissioned in December following : Major Alexander Chisholm, Captain William Bell, Captain Samuel
Sherwood, Captain George W. Myers, Lieutenant
Matthias Marsh, Lieutenant Gilbert Harris, Lieutenant
John Stuart, Lieutenant John Chisholm, Lieutenant
John Fairman, Sen., Lieutenant L. W. Myers, Ensigns
David Simmons, Jacob W. Myers, Alexander Chisholm, Robert Fairman, Samuel B. Gilbert, Adjutant

William Bell, Quarter Master John McIntosh. At the commencement of the War of 1812 John Ferguson, of Kingston, was Colonel ; William Bell, of Thurlow, Lieutenant-Colonel, and Alexander Chisholm, Robert Fairman, Simon McNabb, T. B. Gilbert, Jacob W. Myers, L. W. Myers, David Simmons, Gilbert Harris, and John McIntosh, were Captains of 1st Regiment of Hastings Militia. John Thompson, who had been a soldier in the King's Rangers, was Major.

Dr. Scadding, in his "Toronto of Old," says, "We are informed by Mr. Adiel Sherwood, that James Breakenridge, who had been an officer in Roger's Corps, was appointed the first Lieutenant of the County of Leeds under Simcoe, with authority to organize the body and appoint the officers. Mr. Sherwood received his first commission from him, to the 1st Regiment of Leeds Militia in 1796."

From all this it would appear that at the very threshold of Upper Canada's first emerging into a separate and distinct province, the governing power was alive to the importance of having a well-trained body of militia to defend the country in times of peril from without or within. The same spirit which animated her people in 1812 existed in Simcoe's time, and in Russell's time. To this may be attributed her success in the many engagements which took place in the War of 1812. President Russell laid down the reins of power in 1799, and Governor Hunter reigned in his stead for a period of six years.

Peter Hunter, lately appointed Governor of the province, arrived in York harbour in the *Speedy* in August, 1799. The Niagara *Constellation* of August 23rd, 1799, had in it this notice of the Governor's arrival. It said : " His Excellency Governor Hunter arrived at York on Friday morning last, in the *Speedy*. On landing he was received by a party of the Queen's Rangers ; and at one o'clock, p.m., was waited on at His Honour's, the President's, by the military officers, and congratulated on his safe arrival and appointment to the government of the province."

Governor Hunter did not become at once on his arrival a permanent resident of York. He was not Governor only but Commander-in-Chief of His Majesty's forces in the province as well. His duties as Commander-in-Chief called him shortly after his first arrival away from the Capital to which he did not return till the following May, 1800. The *Gazette* of Saturday, May 17th, had in it this paragraph giving notice of his arrival : " On Thursday evening last (May 15th) His Excellency Peter Hunter, Esquire, Lieutenant-Governor and Commander-in-Chief of this province, arrived in our harbour on board the *Toronto*, and on Friday morning, about nine o'clock, landed at the garrison, where he is at present to reside." Called away from the Capital again, after having opened and closed the Fourth Session of the Second Parliament of the province he returned to 'Quebec, the head-quarters of the King's troops in Canada. This session of the parliament, opened on the 2nd June, 1800, was a short one. Only six Acts were passed, the most important of which were : "An Act for the further introduction of the Criminal Law of England into this province, and for the more effectual punishment of certain offenders," and "An Act for making a temporary provision for the regulation of trade between this province and the United States of America, by land or by inland navigation." On May 16th, in the following year, Governor Hunter arrives again in the *Toronto* from Quebec. The *Gazette* of May 16th, 1801, says, "Arrived this morning on board the *Toronto*, Captain Earl, His Excellency, the Lieutenant-Governor and Secretary, from Quebec."

This visit was doubtless preparatory to the opening of the First Session of the Third Provincial Parliament, which took place on July 9th, 1801. The writs for this parliament were issued on or about the 20th June, 1801. In the *Oracle* of the 20th June, 1801, there appeared an advertisement, signed by William Allan, as Returning Officer for the County of Durham, the East Riding of the County of York and the County of Simcoe, which territories conjointly are to elect one member.   Mr. Allan announces that he will be in attendance "on Thursday, the 2nd day of July next, at ten o'clock in the forenoon, at the Hustings, under the colonnade of the parliament buildings in the Town of York, and proceed to the election of one Knight to represent the said county, riding and county in the House of Assembly, whereof all the freeholders of the said county, riding and county are to take notice." The writ, issuing from His Excellency, Peter Hunter, Esquire, directs the returning officer to cause one Knight, girt with a sword, the most fit and discreet, to be freely and indifferently chosen by those who shall be present on the day of election.   At this period of Upper Canadian parliamentary history, the voters were few and widely scattered.   There were two candidates who presented themselves to the electors, Mr. A. Macdonell and Mr. J. Small.   There were only 144 votes polled, and Mr. Macdonell was elected by a majority of eighty.

Governor Hunter was a military man, and not to be trifled with by officials, whether of high or low degree.   He had not been long in office as Governor when he was waited upon by a deputation of Quakers from the Quaker settlement to the north of York, who came into town to complain to him of the delay which they and their co-religionists had experienced in obtaining the patents for their lands.   Dr. Scadding relates that the Governor "received them in the garrison, and hearing how coming to York on former occasions they had been sent about from one office to another for a reply to their enquiries about the patents, he requested them to come to him the next day at noon. Orders were at the same instant despatched to Mr. D. W. Smith, the Surveyor-General, to Mr. Small, Clerk of the Crown, and to Mr. Jarvis, Secretary and Registrar of the province (all of whom, it appeared, at one time or another had failed to reply satisfactorily to the Quakers), to wait at the same house on the Lieutenant-Governor, bringing with them, each respectively, such papers and memoranda as might be in their possession having relation to patents for lands in Whitchurch and King." "These gentlemen complain," the Governor said, pointing to the Quakers, "that they cannot get their patents." Each of the official personages present offered in succession some indistinct observations, expressive, it would seem, of a degree of regret, and hinted exculpatory reasons, so far as he individually was concerned. On closer interrogation one thing came out very clearly, that the order for the patents was more than twelve months old.

At length the onus of blame seemed to settle down on the head of the Secretary and Registrar, Mr Jarvis, who could only say that really the pressure of business in his office was so great that he had been absolutely unable, up to the present moment, to get ready the particular patents referred to. "Sir," was the Governor's immediate rejoinder, "if they are not forthcoming, every one of them, and placed in the hands of these gentlemen here, at noon on Thursday next (it was now Tuesday), by George, I'll un-Jarvis you!" It is needless to say that by noon of the following Thursday the patents were got ready, and placed in the hands of the Quakers, who returned to their homes with the conviction that the Province had a firm, vigorous and just Governor. Governor Hunter lived long enough to be able to open the first session of the Fourth Parliament of the Province, which was opened on the first day of February, 1805. The election of this Parliament was an exciting one. Heretofore candidates had been principally of the official class, for at this time place men were eligible for a seat in the House of Assembly. Mr. Joseph Willcocks was sheriff and member of Parliament. He lost his office of sheriff by giving a vote contrary to the policy of the Lieutenant-Governor for the time being. He was returned as a member of the House of Assembly, and after having been imprisoned for breach of privilege he was returned again and continued to lead the party of Reform. In Governor Hunter's time Independent candidates were just beginning to come forward to do battle with the official class. In the election of 1804 to send representatives to the fourth Parliament, commencing in 1805, three candidates presented themselves to the electors of the east riding of York and asked their suffrages. The three candidates were Mr. A. Macdonell, Mr. D. W. Smith, and Mr. Weeks. The last named was Independent and for reform. As was to be expected, he lost his election, the official being elected. He was more successful in 1806, when he was returned for the same constituency.- He did not long enjoy his honours, being killed in a duel in the same year. In the *Oracle* of 11th October, 1806, the following notice appeared : " Died, on Friday, the 10th instant, in consequence of a wound received that morning in a duel, William Weeks, Esq., Barrister-at-Law and Member of the House of Assembly for the Counties of York, Durham and Simcoe."

The administration of the affairs of the Province by Governor Hunter may be said to have been eminently successful. He was an officer of unblemished reputation. As a man and as Governor he was firm, resolute, just, and of unswerving integrity. He died at Quebec, on the 23rd August, 1805. In the *Oracle* for September 28th, 1805, appeared the following notice of his character : " As an officer his character was high and unsullied ; and at this moment his death may be considered a great public loss. As Lieutenant-Governor of Upper Canada his loss will be severely felt ; for by his unremitting attention and exertions he has in the course of a few years brought that infant colony to an unparalleled state of prosperity."

Alexander Grant, Esquire, on the death of Governor Hunter, as senior member of the Executive Council, was President of the Province until the arrival of Governor Yonge in 1807. Mr. Grant, afterwards well known as Commodore Grant, held the office for so short a time that we can only make a brief reference to his administration. He opened Parliament on the 4th February, 1805, and prorogued the session on 2nd March, 1806. The Parliament during his administration appropriated £800 for the purchase of instruments for illustrating the principles of Natural Philosophy. The instruments were purchased, and all, or nearly all, found their way into the Home District School. President Grant, in his speech at the close of the session of 1806, alluded to the action of Parliament in the following terms : " The encouragement which you have given for procuring the means necessary for communicating useful and ornamental knowledge to the rising generation meets with my approbation, and I have no doubt will produce the most salutary effects."

From the foregoing it will be seen that while Major-General Simcoe was serving the Crown in other quarters, the executive affairs of the Province were administered by two presidents and one governor, the latter a military man.

MONUMENT TO GENERAL SIMCOE.

Photographed from the Memorial Tablet in Exeter Cathedral.

CHAPTER XIII.

St. Domingo and the Portuguese Mission.

IN order to have a correct understanding of this mission of Governor Simcoe to St. Domingo (or as it is now called Hayti), it is fit, if not necessary, to give some account of the causes which led the British Government to vest in him the command of her forces in that island.

The island was, after its first discovery by Christopher Columbus (1492) down to 1698, a Spanish possession, the largest and most valuable of the West India Islands, and known to the world under the Spanish name of Hispaniola. The island is in length more than 450 miles from east to west, and 150 in breadth. Columbus, in his voyage of discovery in 1492, landed at a small bay which he called St. Nicholas, and then named the island Espagnola, in honour of the country by whose king he was employed. St. Domingo, by the treaties of Aix-la-Chapelle and Nimeguen in 1668 and 1678, was partitioned between the French and the Spaniards with no more regular

boundaries established than a custom, constantly sub-
jected to change from a variety of circumstances. The
peace of Ryswick in 1668 afforded the first regular
cession of the western part of the island to the French,
which, however, formed a very small part of the island,
not more than a fourth part of the whole dependency.
The whole island abounds in fertility of soil, rich in all
tropical products, and was a most valuable accession to
the kingdoms of France and Spain. The French
colony, with fewer national advantages, presented a
marked contrast to the inactivity of the neighbouring
country, and procured for it a character almost equal
to that which has been so generally given to the whole
of the island at its discovery, which Columbus described
as the *original seat of Paradise*, and Edwards in his
historical survey in describing the western or French
part of the island "the garden of the West Indies,
which, for beautiful scenery, richness of soil, salubrity
and variety of climate, might justly be deemed the
paradise of the new world." Port-au-Prince was the
ostensible metropolis of the French colony, and the
seat of its government ; except in time of war, when it
was removed to Cape François. The inhabitants of
the island were composed of pure whites, people of
colour, blacks of free condition, and negroes in a state
of slavery. The whole of the intermediate grades were
called generally mulattoes. The French Revolution of

1789 extended its ramifications through the whole French Empire, including its distant colonies. St. Domingo did not escape the contagion. Restlessness and contempt of authority seized upon the islanders black and white. There were in the island revolutionists, republicans, monarchists, and people so vicious as to be prepared to enter upon any enterprise which might gain them notoriety of a good or bad character. In 1791 the slaves rose in rebellion, which threatened an overthrow of the French Government and general conflagration. The authorities sent commissioners to the British Island of Jamaica to request the assistance of troops, arms, ammunition and provisions, when Admiral Affleck ordered the *Blonde* and the *Daphne* frigates to repair to St. Domingo to overawe the insurgents. Some time after this an armament was formed at Jamaica, composed of the 13th Regiment of Foot, seven companies of the 49th Regiment and a detachment of artillery, furnishing about eight hundred and seventy rank and file. With the first division of these, consisting of about six hundred and seventy-nine rank and file, Lieut.-Colonel Whitlock arrived at Jeremie on the 19th of September, 1793, and took possession of the town and harbour on the following morning. British colours were hoisted on the forts with royal salutes, and the inhabitants swore allegiance to Great Britain.

The British continued to give aid and comfort to the French authorities, obtained possession of many forts and fortified places, and ultimately captured the capital, Port-au-Prince.   Shortly after the capture of the capital that dread disease yellow fever attacked the troops, decimating the force which up to this time had done noble service in quelling the insurrection—in a measure restoring tranquillity and exhibiting the force and power of British arms.   From the time that the yellow fever set in till the spring of 1796 the aspect of affairs began to change.   The insurrectionists, commanded by a very able general, taking advantage of the deplorable condition of the British troops, attacked the outposts of the British and regained lost ground. So languid became the progress of the British arms that the Republicans of the island, aided by the blacks and mulattoes, commenced operations in every quarter round the capital ; besides compelling General Forbes to fortify the mountain called Grenier, and to occupy all the surrounding heights, they employed some months in the erection of batteries, and on the fortifications of two forts at St. Laurent and Le Boutilliere, within five miles of Port-au-Prince, without the smallest molestation from the English.

"Affairs becoming desperate," says Rainsford in his history of Hayti, "with misfortune and experience, the Government determined on sending General Simcoe to endeavour to recover the British character; and if experience and skill were all that were wanting, little doubt could have been entertained of success. He arrived at St. Nicholas Mole in the beginning of March, 1797, and immediately proceeded through the British possessions to discover the evil, before the application of the remedies with which he was so well acquainted. But alas! no ordinary remedies were applicable to the desperate circumstances which he had to encounter; for, instructed in the science of government and the relation of empires, by the inconsistency of one power and improved in the art of war by the impolicy of the other, the blacks had arrived at a degree of perfection in both, that, notwithstanding the inveteracy of prejudice, compelled itself to be accredited by its effects. An acknowledgment of this fact incontestably took place the same month, in which the command of the British army was confided to the wisdom and activity of General Simcoe, by the appointment of Toussaint L'Overture, the celebrated negro officer, by the French Government to be General-in-Chief of the armies in St. Domingo. General Simcoe commenced several economical arrangements, which, even if his cause was hopeless, could not fail to render it admirable service. He compelled a surrender of all private leases obtained of the vacated property of French absentees, to the public use; he reformed the Colonial Corps, placing on a temporary half-pay the officers necessarily withdrawn, and rendering more eligible those who were the fittest for service. . . . Toussaint adopted every mode to harass him, and turn the war in his own favour, by every stratagem that could be devised. He menaced the important frontier post of Mireballais, which had been erected with stone at considerable expense ; the commandant immediately evacuated it, and retired to Port-au-Prince, leaving the rich plain of the Cul de Sac open to the enemy, thereby impeding the communication of the English with Banica and Spanish St. Domingo. With somewhat of spirit, and better success, the batteries which had insulted the capital were carried ; they required, however, a body of two thousand blacks, besides a reserve of British troops and some artillery, and cost the life of a brave officer of colour, as he was leading the charge at St. Laurent, Major Pouchet.

"While these operations employed the vicinity of the capital, Rigaud was active in his quarter. With one thousand two hundred men he attacked the post at Irois, and gave the first notice of his approach by his fire on the fort. The fort was composed of a battalion of black troops under Colonel De Grasse, a company of British under Lieutenant Talbot and twenty black artillery under M. de Brueil.

"Fortunately the artillery of Rigaud was interrupted by Captain Rickets, of the *Magicienne* frigate,

which caused him to retire precipitately. To increase
the eclat of the repulse, another immediately followed,
of Toussaint, from the Town of St. Marc; it was a
repulse, nevertheless, dearly bought.

"Wearied with the kind of warfare in which he
was thus unavailingly engaged, General Simcoe returned to England in August (1797) to procure a force
sufficient to pursue a career of glory, or to abandon
a scene furnishing at best but negative honours.

"The ministry of Great Britain were employed in
the complicated affairs of Europe too much to give
more attention to St. Domingo, and General Whyte
supplied the place of General Simcoe with no additional means of success."

Rainsford, in his account of the proceedings in
St. Domingo adds this note referring to Major-General
Simcoe: "The writer cannot omit in this place paying
his tribute of respect to this excellent and gallant
officer. If all the abilities of the General, the suavity
of the gentleman, and the vigorous powers of a manly
understanding may be expected to unite in one person,
it is in Lieutenant-General Simcoe. When commanding the Queen's Rangers, in the American War, he
distinguished himself on every occasion, and in a
variety of important battles crowned himself and his
corps with the highest military glory."

In executing his mission to St. Domingo, Governor Simcoe was as successful as the condition of the Island and its affairs would admit. In October, 1798, not long after his return to England, he was made a Lieutenant-General in the British Army.

During the time that Simcoe was in St. Domingo, serving the English as their General, and commander of their forces, at the same time assisting the French to maintain their authority in the island, Napoleon Bonaparte was rising into distinction and power in France. He was then only twenty-seven years of age, but was second in command of her army as an officer of artillery. Before the year (1796) was over Napoleon had become Commander-in-Chief of the army of France. He had no sooner attained supreme authority in the army than he undertook the subjugation of Italy, which he succeeding in effecting. The Siege of Mantua was undertaken, the bridge of Lodi was passed, and Italy became subject to the rule of the French. · Mr. Pitt was still in power in England, and was being severely criticised for carrying on a war with France, a country which was in a state of revolution within itself. Mr. Fox denounced the war as a folly and an injustice to the tax-payers of England, who were called upon to pay the expense. Still England was so enraged at the successes of Napoleon on the Continent that she determined the war must continue. Soon England's wooden walls are shaken by a mutiny in the fleet. The mutiny is suppressed and by-and-by Admiral Jervis, seconded by Nelson and Collingwood, gain a signal naval victory over the Spanish at Cape St. Vincent. This victory delivered England from all fear of invasion and inspired her people with fresh courage.

Although England was victorious on the water, France was pushing her successes on the Continent. In twenty days after the opening of the campaign of 1797 Bonaparte had driven the Archduke Charles of Austria over the Alps. Next he attacks and defeats the Venetians, and at the close of the year is covered with glory and conquest.

It is a singular circumstance, and only goes to prove the magnanimity of England, that while she was at war with France she was at the same time endeavouring to assist the French in quelling a rebellion in one of her colonies. But then it must be taken into account that England, in giving aid to the French in St. Domingo, was seconding the efforts of the ruling powers of St. Domingo who were as much opposed to Napoleon and Republicanism as was England herself.

In the spring of 1798 Napoleon invades Egypt, attacks and defeats the Mamelukes. Now comes the Battle of the Nile and the great naval victory of Admiral Lord Nelson. This was a sad blow and great discouragement to the great Napoleon. Still he was enabled to cross the desert, and with an army of sixteen thousand men invade Syria, make an attack on and suffer a defeat at the hands of Sir Sydney Smith.

In 1799 Napoleon is First Consul of France, exercising despotic sway. On the 24th December a new Constitution is proclaimed, a new revolution had been effected, and France was in the hands of a military chieftain. The First Consul thought it the interest of France to offer peace to Great Britain, who was much too troublesome in meeting the designs and ambitions of the great General. Mr. Pitt, however, would not make peace with a revolutionary power. In 1800 Bonaparte made his celebrated passage over the Alps and gained a signal victory at Marengo. In March, 1802, the Peace of Amiens was signed, which gave to France a great accession of territory, the possession of Belgium, and the whole left bank of the Rhine. The years 1803-1804 were comparatively uneventful, but early in 1805 the three great European Powers, England, Austria and Russia, entered into a coalition with the purpose of curbing the power of Napoleon. The French Emperor—for by this time Napoleon had become Emperor of France—had thought of invading England ; he was, however, thwarted in this enterprise. He then turned his attention to Austria ; but before his armies could meet in Germany, Nelson had gained the great naval victory of Trafalgar, by which the naval power of France and Spain was so crippled that England remained during the continuance of the war mistress of the ocean.

On the 1st of December, 1805, the battle of Austerlitz was fought. This great battle, in which Napoleon was completely successful, added greatly to his glory and renown. Austria, humbled by the Emperor, entered into negotiations for peace, which were concluded by treaty at Presburg, on the 27th December, 1805. Alas! the success of Napoleon at Austerlitz so affected the spirits of the great statesman Pitt that he sank under the disastrous intelligence; he died on the 23rd January, 1806, at the age of forty-seven. His great rival, Fox, only survived him a few months; he died on the 13th September following.

The intention of the French, that is, of Napoleon Bonaparte, to invade Portugal had for some time been manifest in various ways during the summer of 1806, and it appeared to the English Government that the situation of that country was becoming critical. It was felt that if France should succeed in establishing a peace with the northern powers she would probably attack the only remaining ally of England upon the Continent, and might even succeed in making herself mistress of the Portuguese dominions.

Portugal, from its long alliance with England, was regarded almost as a part of the English dominions, both in a commercial and political point of view. Considerable as were the benefits England derived from its trade, and great as was the preponderance of England in its councils, the British people certainly formed an exaggerated estimate of both. Seizing upon Portugal was like a direct defeat of England.

Bonaparte was smarting under the recent defeat at Trafalgar, and had found not the least facility in his plans of invasion, so that anything like a territorial advantage over England would be a gratification, if it did not amount to a compensation.

The possession of the Tagus was intimately connected with our other great naval victory at St. Vincent; but, though the importance of that event in rescuing England from the most complicated and most inextricable embarrassments must have been well known to him, he cared little about anything that had happened before in his own reign, so entirely did personal vanity form a part of his character, more entirely than of any other person of great renown. To be able to boast that he had driven the English into the sea, captured their only stronghold on the Continent, and dethroned those who held it by and for them was his main object, and probably nearer his heart than any substantial injury done to England or any real advantage gained to himself.

The courts, too, both at Lisbon and Madrid, were

feeble beyond all description ; their Governments, both civil and ecclesiastical, as bad as possible ; the Queen of Portugal and the Prince of Peace (her favourite minister Godoy) more likely to assist the French in destroying Portugal than to oppose any obstacle to its destruction. Since the Peace of Presburg, Bonaparte had nothing to occupy his attention, nor had anything occurred to postpone the object—subduing the ally of England and winning Gibraltar, the last stake England had to lose on the Continent of Europe.

Early in August, 1806, the English Government had received intelligence of the intention of France to invade Portugal with an army of thirty thousand men, then assembled at Bayonne. From perfectly reliable information it was believed that the object and intention of Bonaparte was to dethrone the Royal Family and to partition Portgual, allotting one part to Spain and the other to the Prince of Peace or to the Queen of Etruria.

The ministers, therefore, resolved to send an army to the Tagus, to be there met by a competent naval force, the whole to be entrusted to the command of Lord St. Vincent and Lieutenant-General Simcoe, with full powers, conjointly with Lord Rosslyn, to negotiate with the Court of Lisbon.

Mr. Brougham received from the Foreign Office the following letter :—

" Downing Street,

" August 12th, 1806.

" Sir,—I am directed by Mr. Secretary Fox to inform you that His Majesty having been pleased to appoint the Earl of Rosslyn, the Earl of St. Vincent, and Lieutenant-General Simcoe to proceed on a special mission to the Court of Lisbon, you have been selected to accompany them as Secretary to the said mission. You will thereupon join the Earl of Rosslyn and General Simcoe, who are proceeding without delay to the place of their destination, where the Earl of St. Vincent will be already arrived, and place yourself under their directions ; and you will exert yourself to the best of your ability in the execution of such matters as may be entrusted to you.

" Benj. Tucker."

Mr. Brougham was further informed that to avoid multiplying places unnecessarily he was named Secretary, but in all other respects he was to act as a fourth Commissioner.

Mr. Brougham, than whom no one could speak with more knowledge of the circumstances and of the men with whom he was associated as Secretary and fourth Commissioner, has, in his Memoirs, borne testimony to the fitness of his fellow Commissioner. He says :—" The three Commissioners were as well selected as possible for this delicate and difficult service. The Admiral's name, renowned all over the world, was particularly an object of veneration in these countries which had witnessed his great exploits. Of the Generals, Lord Rosslyn had served in the country and was distinguished by his great knowledge and talent for business ; and the third one, General Simcoe, son of that great captain of the navy who had been sent to Lisbon at the time of the great earthquake with the liberal grant of money, given to relieve the distress which it had occasioned."

Major-General Simcoe was taken ill on the voyage undertaken to execute the mission to Portugal, and his malady increased so rapidly that he was under the necessity of speedily returning to England where he died shortly after his arrival. In the *Upper Canada Gazette or American Chronicle*, under date of February 7th, 1807, was published the following notice as a communication from London :—

" LONDON, November 6th, 1806.

"General Simcoe, we regret to state, died on Tuesday last, at Topham, in Devonshire. He arrived at Torbay a few days before, and was conveyed from thence by water to Topham."

It now only remains to say that it is hoped that a suitable monument may be erected to the memory of Upper Canada's first Governor, in some public place in the Province, a fitting tribute to the memory of a truly great man and worthy Governor. The date of his death and some of his many virtues are recorded on a monument erected to his memory in Exeter Cathedral.

The legend upon this monument is in the following words :—

SACRED TO THE MEMORY

OF

JOHN GRAVES SIMCOE,

LIEUTENANT-GENERAL IN THE ARMY, AND COLONEL OF THE 22ND REGIMENT OF FOOT,

Who died on the 25th day of October, 1806,

AGED 54 YEARS,

IN WHOSE LIFE AND CHARACTER THE VIRTUES OF THE HERO, THE PATRIOT, AND THE CHRISTIAN WERE SO EMINENTLY CONSPICUOUS, THAT IT MAY BE JUSTLY SAID, HE SERVED HIS KING AND HIS COUNTRY WITH A ZEAL EXCEEDED ONLY BY HIS PIETY TOWARD GOD.

Above this inscription is a medallion portrait. On the right and left are figures of an Indian and a soldier of the Queen's Rangers.

APPENDIX.

ACT OF 1792 FOUNDED ON IMPERIAL CONSTITUTIONAL ACT OF 1791.

N Act to repeal certain parts of an Act passed in the fourteenth year of His Majesty's reign, intituled "An Act for making more effectual provision for the Government of the Province of Quebec, in North America," and to introduce the English law as the rule of decision in all matters of controversy relative to property and civil rights.

[Passed 15th October, 1792.]

WHEREAS, by an Act passed in the fourteenth year of His present Majesty, intituled "An Act for making more effectual provision for the Government of the Province of Quebec, in North America," it was among other things provided, that in all matters of controversy relative to property and civil rights, resort should be had to the laws of Canada as the rule for the decision of the same, such provision being manifestly and avowedly intended for the accommodation of His Majesty's Canadian subjects;

And whereas, since the passing of the Act aforesaid, that part of the late Province of Quebec now comprehended within the Province of Upper Canada, having become inhabited principally by British subjects, born and educated where the English laws were established, and who are unaccustomed to the laws of Canada, it is inexpedient that the provision aforesaid, contained in the said Act of the fourteenth year of His present

Majesty, should be continued in this Province. Be it enacted by the King's Most Excellent Majesty, by and with the advice and consent of the Legislative Council and Assembly of the Province of Upper Canada, constituted and assembled by virtue of, and under the authority of, an Act passed in the Parliament of Great Britain, intituled " An Act to repeal certain parts of an Act passed in the fourteenth year of His Majesty's reign, intituled ' An Act for making more effectual provision for the Government of the Province of Quebec, in North America,' and to make further provision for the government of the said Province," and it is hereby enacted, that from and after the passing of this Act, the said provision contained in the said Act of the fourteenth year of His present Majesty, be and the same is hereby repealed ; and the authority of the said laws of Canada, and every part thereof, as forming a rule of decision in all matters of controversy relative to property and civil rights shall be annulled, made void and abolished throughout this Province, and that the said laws, nor any part thereof as such shall be of any force or authority within the said Province, nor binding on any of the inhabitants thereof.

II. Provided always, and be it enacted by the authority aforesaid, that nothing in this Act shall extend to extinguish, release or discharge, or otherwise to affect any existing right, lawful claim or incumbrance to and upon any lands, tenements or hereditaments within the said Province, or to rescind or vacate, or otherwise to affect any contract or security already made and executed conformably to the usages prescribed by the said laws of Canada.

III. And be it further enacted by the authority aforesaid, that from and after the passing of this Act in all matters of controversy and civil rights resort shall be had to the laws of England as the rule for the decision of the same.

IV. Provided always, and be it enacted by the authority aforesaid, that nothing in this Act shall extend, or be construed to extend, to repeal or vary any of the ordinances made and passed by the Governor and Legislative Council of the Province of Quebec previous to the division of the same into the Provinces of Upper and Lower Canada, otherwise than as they are necessarily varied by the provisions hereinafter mentioned.

V. And be it further enacted by the authority aforesaid, that all matters relative to testimony and legal proof in the investigation of fact, and the forms thereof in the several Courts of Law and Equity within this Province, be regulated by the rules of evidence established in England.

VI. Provided always, and be it enacted by the authority aforesaid, that nothing in this Act contained shall vary or interfere, or be construed to vary or interfere with any of the existing provisions respecting ecclesiastical rights or dues within this Province or with the forms of proceeding in civil actions, or the jurisdiction of the Courts already established, or to introduce any of the laws of England respecting the maintenance of the poor, or respecting bankrupts.

CPSIA information can be obtained
at www.ICGtesting.com
Printed in the USA
FSHW021821080319
56181FS

9 781407 753164